Tricia Sturgeon lives in a coastal village in North Norfolk and in the past has written for *My Weekly* magazine, *The Friendship Book*, and has had works published in the *Daily Mail*. She has also appeared on BBC Radio Norfolk several times to read her poetry.

All royalties received by the author for this book will be given to animal charities.

Cockleshells
A Book of People Poetry

Tricia Sturgeon

Cockleshells

A Book of People Poetry

Vanguard Press

VANGUARD PAPERBACK

© Copyright 2014
Tricia Sturgeon

A CIP catalogue record for this title is
available from the British Library.

ISBN: 978-1-84386-745-6

*Vanguard Press is an imprint of
Pegasus Elliot MacKenzie Publishers Ltd.*
www.pegasuspublishers.com

First Published in 2014

**Vanguard Press
Sheraton House Castle Park
Cambridge England**

Printed & Bound in Great Britain

To all who have walked with me.

May I take just a moment to thank you, my dears
For all of your friendship, through all of the years.
For giving me knowledge when I didn't know
For planting the seeds so that the wisdom could grow.
For a shoulder to lean on, for showing you care,
For sharing your laughter, for just "being there".
For giving me strength when I'd none of my own
For letting me know I was never alone.
For all you have brought me of loving and caring
For all you have taught me of giving and sharing.
For helping me carve, with an everyday knife
The shape of my soul, from the granite of life.

Contents

I   **17**

DREAMING

DREAMING…?   19
DECADES   21
MISTS OF TIME   24
EMBERS   26
COSMIC REQUESTS   28
YOU TELL ME YOU SEE FAIRIES   30
BLUEBELLS   33
ANGELS   35

II   **39**

GENERAL AND NARRATIVE POEMS

RICHES   41
OPPOSITES ATTRACT   42
MAGIC   44
FALLEN ANGELS   47
REBIRTH   49
ALCHEMY   51
BEGGAR-MY-NEIGHBOUR   53
DANDELION   55
THE PICTURE   56
TRANSITION   58
THE BINDING   60

THE SHIP	62
RICH MAN, POOR MAN	65
PUT OUT THE STARS	67
TRANSFORMATION	69
CHIMES	71
IT'S MRS TOMMY JOHNSON, GOD...	72
THE ALMIGHTY DOLLAR	75
LOST	77
JENNY'S TEA	79
COMMUNION	81
FEED THE BIRDS...	82
"MISTICAL" MORN	83
TICK TOCK	84
TRANSFORMATION	85
DELIGHT	86
GIVING THANKS	87
SPIRALS	89
WAR AND PEACE	90
COURAGE...	92
PICTURES	94
SEEDLINGS	96
WHO MADE THE MUSIC?	97
QUESTIONS	99
PERFECT RECALL	100
SNOOZIN'	101
DON'T BLAME POOR OLD MONEY.	102
SHIFTING SHAPE	104

III

HUMOROUS

107

AGE BEFORE BEAUTY 109

OVERTAKEN 110

NO CONTEST 112

HOLIDAY POSTCARD 114

RISE ABOVE IT… 116

HEALTHY EATING 118

COBWEBS 120

THE RUMMAGE SALE 122

TIME – LESS 124

THE QUEUE 125

OTHER PEOPLE'S PLATES 127

HIDE AND SEEK 129

IV

COMFORT

131

LOVE SURVIVES 133

DON'T WEEP FOR ME 134

TIME 136

CIRCLES 137

NOT JUST TODAY 138

FAMILY 139

DON'T ASK ME TO STAY… 141

TOUGH LOVE 143

PRAYING 145

REUNION 147

CROSSING THE VOID 149

LOVE NEVER GOES AWAY   150
BECOMING ONE   151

V   153
MORE GENERAL AND NARRATIVE POEMS
THE BAG LADY   155
WARRIORS   157
IF YOU WISH…   158
WRINKLES…   159
WRITTEN IN THE STARS   160
GIFT OF LOVE   161
PAGES…   162
THE HEALER   163
MASQUE   164
BLACK VELVET   165
UNDERSTANDING   166
TOMORROW   168
TOGETHERNESS   169
TRUE LOVE   171
THINKING OF YOU…   173
THE THIEF   174
TESSIE   176
TEARS…   178
TIME AND TIDE   179
SYMBIOSIS   180
THE HOME STRAIGHT   182
WHEN YOU WISH…   183
THE LESSER SPOTTED SOUL   184

ALL THE TIME IN THE WORLD	185
SPECIAL	186
RAINY DAYS	187
SNOWDROP	188
SKY-BORNE	189
SKETCHES	190
SIGHTS UNSEEN	192
SEAGULLS	194
SEASONS	195
SAINTS ALIVE	197
WELCOME HOME	199
RUSHING ALONG…	200
RESCUE	201
RAINBOW	202
QUIET TIME	203
PRESENT COMPANY	204
HAD I THE POWER…	205
PLAYMATES	206
ADORNMENT	208
PATTERNS	209
OH GOD…!	210
ONE O'CLOCK, TWO O'CLOCK…	212
NO MAN'S LAND	213
NIGHT TERRORS	215
TREASURE HUNT	216
BY ANY OTHER NAME…	218
MORNING GLORY	219
MOTHER OF PEARL	220
MIRROR IMAGE	222

MILLIE'S GIFT	223
ME?	224
MAGIC	226
LOVE IS…	228
LOVE…	229
LIGHT FANTASTIC	230
LEFT BEHIND…	231
I DID NOT KNOW…	233
JIM	234
I WISH FOR YOU…	236
INCARNATION	237
HOPE	239
HIGH AND MIGHTY	240
GUARDIAN	241
GROWING PAINS	242
FUGITIVES	244
BUT THEN FACE TO FACE…	245
FOOTSTEPS…	247
AFTER THE RAIN	248
FRIENDS…	249
MY FRIEND	250
DISCOVERY	251
ANGEL EXPRESS…	252
NEW YEAR'S EVE	254
ENDURANCE	256
ELIXIR	257
ELEMENTAL	258
POINT OF DEPARTURE	259
DAFFODILS	261

CONCRETE EVIDENCE 263

MORTAL'S COMBATS 264

THE BURDEN… 265

ALL THINGS BRIGHT AND… 266

BUILDING BLOCKS… 269

BEING… 271

BEGUILED… 272

BECAUSE… 273

BEAUTY 274

AUTUMNAL ANTICS 276

ALL TOGETHER NOW… 277

CAST IRON LOVE 279

NEVER 280

ANGELS UNAWARE 281

AMBER'S SONG 283

THE LONELY JOURNEY 284

ANGELIC FRIENDS 286

ADVICE 288

FOR 'KENZIE, MADDIE, 288

AND DIXIE-MAY 288

PHOTO OF A DEAR FRIEND 290

FEATHERED FRIENDS 291

EVERYTHING CHANGES 292

I

Dreaming

Dreaming...?

Last night, I had a great and wondrous dream
…yet did I sleep?
So real did all things seem
That even now, in brightest day, I feel
Its awesome power
To liberate and heal.

Come dearest friends, and hear my tale, draw near
For I have words
To banish dread and fear
Words which I could ne'er have known, except
An angel knelt beside me
And whispered as I slept.
An angel robed in beauty, joy and grace
With love's compassion
Etched upon his face.

"Who are you, shining one," I breathed "and why
Have you begged leave
To visit from on high?"
"My child," he said. "I am your greatest friend

And you will find me
Waiting at the end
Of life's rough road.
I'll catch your final breath
And hold you close
My name is Death."

"But you are clad in love and peace," I said.
"While Death comes draped
In misery and dread."
"Dear child," he answered… tender was his smile.
"I wear those garments
For a little while,
To hold you close, within in my dark disguise
Lest Heaven's light
Should hurt your eyes."

Decades

When I was five, why, time stood still
Well, hardly moved at all,
As the magic of each moment
Held me tight within its thrall.
The ticking clock could not be heard
In nursery or den.
I could not comprehend a year,
Much less a year times ten.

In time, in time, in lots of time
A decade rolled away,
As countless brim-full, stretchy hours
Made up each endless day.
With fifteen years inside my skin
And growing still to do,
The world seemed like a shiny toy,
Still half unwrapped, brand new.

By twenty-five, I found that time
Had quickened to a trot,
And sometimes got in front of me,
A little… not a lot.
By and large I felt that I
Retained the upper hand,
For days spread out ahead of me
Like sun-kissed grains of sand.

And, oh my dears, by thirty-five
I hadn't time to breathe.
I worked and played so hard that you
Would simply not believe
The "stuff" I packed into each day,
Each evening, every night.
If time's thread dared to fray,
I tied a knot, and held on tight.

By forty-five, I knew that I
Would have to get a grip.
That time was far too precious a resource
To just let slip.
I knew the clock was out there,
For I heard its distant chime.
I vowed to make each minute count…
As soon as I had time!

At fifty-five, on taking stock,
I felt I must concede
I wasn't going to win the race
For time was in the lead.
But cunningly decided that
With just a bit of luck,
I'd stop his headlong gallop
With a little nip and tuck.

Alas, the years took little heed
And sped along apace,
Ignoring all the 'anti-age'
I rubbed into my face.
I took up yoga, learned tai chi,
The same old war was waged,
For sixty-five, I told myself,
Was merely middle-aged.

And still the Earth turned round and round
As months and years played chase,
Leading me... I see it now...
Right back to my first base,
Where memories of years gone by
Seem near enough to touch.
And from this vantage point, I see
Time doesn't matter much.

Mists of Time

Once upon a time, when I was young,
And all my hopes and dreams were shiny bright,
I knew that I was born to find a way
To forge a path from darkness into light.

I saw myself with armour, sword and shield
Astride a milk white steed, with hooves of gold…
But then I put away my childish dreams
And set about the task of growing old.

Which business was accomplished in a trice,
Well within a blinking of an eye.
The decades mere acquaintances, they came,
Touched my brow, and then just hurried by.

Such years as lie ahead are very few,
Too precious to be squandered on regret.
Tho' memories invade and claim the mind
With echoes of those high ideals unmet.

And yet… and here's the wonder, here's the joy…
Within my heart, that far off light still gleams
For parting mists reveal a milk white steed
Caparisoned in daisy-chains and dreams.

Embers

Something... I know not what... some little thing
Turned my thoughts towards the march of Time,
And all the varied landscapes we traverse
On life's relentless trek, that upward climb.
Musing then, upon those bygone scenes,
And wrapping them in shades of rose and gold,
I marvel at the times the earth has turned
Since our enchanted-summer tale was told.

Sweet memories crowd round about my heart
And whisper soft "Do you remember when..."
And with a sudden shock, I realise
That half my lifetime has been lived since then.
And now I do not know the whys and wherefores
The highs and lows, the rhythm of your days.
I do not know what lights your far horizon,
What hopes sustain your heart, what music plays.

I wonder... do you sometimes think about me?
Perhaps just when I turn my thoughts to you,
Sending fond remembrance o'er the ether,

Hoping that your dreams have all come true.
Our love was bright and wonderful and precious,
And tho' the flames died down, as all flames will,
They left their embers scattered in the corners of my heart
I feel their warmth, for they are glowing still.

Cosmic Requests

Once upon a time, there lived
Long, oh long ago,
Upon a rainbow mountain top
Where turquoise rivers flow,
A weaver of the brightest dreams
A conjurer of spells.
With powers to transform the world
... Or so the legend tells.

And anyone who wanted so
To spread a little joy,
To light some darkling corner
Or find a missing toy,
To heal a hurt or make a smile
Or be a force for good
Could throw their wishes in the air
Just knowing that they would
Fly speedily o'er hill and dale
No matter night or day,
To land upon the mountain top
As soon as right away.

And there, they'd whirl around, around
Like petals in a breeze,
And each would hold a "thank you"
And each would hold a "please".
And each one would be answered
In some quite wondrous way,
Sometimes in a year or two,
And sometimes in a day.

And do you know, and can you guess
What I'm about to tell?
The magic and the mountain
Exist today as well!
No map charts their location
No plane can take us there,
But, as of old, we still may toss
Our wishes in the air.
Then, for sure, somewhere, sometime
Somehow, we will achieve,
Our hopes and dreams and heart's desire
Just wish… and then believe.

You Tell Me You See Fairies

You tell me you see fairies.
Watch them whirl and twirl and fly.
You say I do not see them 'cos
They're very, very shy.
And very, very magical
And very, very wise,
And only ever show themselves
To wide and wondering eyes.
If I sit still beside you
Why then, I may just catch
Their game of Tag or Hide and Seek,
Down by the cabbage patch.

All are clad in spider silk
Newly spun at dawn.
One has just washed out her wings
And looks a bit forlorn.
Their laughter rings like bluebells
Their smiles are sunbeam bright
They play and play the whole long day
And never, ever fight.

By night, they gather moonbeams
All shiny, new and clean
To weave a silver coronet,
A gift for Mab, their Queen.
They dip it in a rainbow
So it shines with every hue
Then spangle it with diamonds
Gleaned from the morning dew.
And elves are mounted on their steeds,
Field mousies, sleek and brown,
Riding forth to gather in
Bags of thistledown,
To fluff the tiny pillows
And the duvets, soft and deep,
To keep the fairies cosy
When they snuggle down to sleep.

You tell me you see fairies
Where I see leaf and stalk.
I hear the wind a-whistling
But you hear fairy talk.
There has to be a reason
And the reason has to be
That I'm a grown up mummy
And you are only three.
And 'ere you leave your childhood
As, little one, you must,
I hope that they will sprinkle you
With silver fairy dust.

Then, with years flown and you all grown
Perhaps, yourself a wife,
You will always see the magic
In the cabbage patch of life.

Bluebells

Oh how I hope this world is blessed
With tiny fairy folk,
Who live within the myriad folds
Of Mother Nature's cloak.
I'm pretty sure they're all around,
And think, perhaps a clue
Lies in the fact that no-one else
Can do what fairies do.
For who would thread a spiders web
With dewy diamond drops,
Or romp with woodland rabbits
On their early morning hops.
Find the plumpest ears of corn
For hungry harvest mice,
Then polish up the ladybirds
To keep them looking nice.
Wake the early worms and teach
The baby frogs to leap,
And every night, make sure that
All the daisies are asleep?
They toss the scents of summer,

Like petals, in the air
So humankind may take delight
In all the fragrance there.
Then gather moon and star-shine to
Weave into magic spells,
And fashion mislaid thimbles
Into useful wishing wells.
Thread rainbows through each puddle,
Plant a perfect toadstool ring
For holding midnight court before
Their fairy queen and king.

So… yes, I'm sure that pixie folk
And elfin sprites abound.
For who would ring a bluebell chime
If fairies weren't around?

Angels

We each have got an angel,
Leastways, that's what I'm told,
Hovering beside us
In robes of white and gold.
Our guide and our protector
From birth, right on through death
As close as every heartbeat,
And near as every breath.

Well now, you know, that isn't right
Nor not exactly fair.
For they should get a fly – about
And tea – breaks here and there.
Well, don't it stand to reason
I mean, for goodness sake
Even the Creator... well,
He had to 'ave a break.

They wouldn't simply leave us
For fear that we might sink.
Instead, they use the services
Of "Acting Angels Inc."
You say you've never 'eard of them?
Oh dear! Where 'ave you been?
They're here and there and everywhere,
Always on the scene.

Mind you, they're incognito.
Quite often in disguise.
And come in many different shapes
And every sort of size.
But they'll come out of hiding
To brighten up the day,
Even knockin' on the door
"To see if you're OK."

That neighbour, offering a lift
To take us in to town,
The arms which give a heavenly hug
When we feel lost and down.
The shoulders that we cry on.
The hands that share our load.
The feet, which keep us company
Along the rocky road.

They're reaching out an' giving
Not waitin' to be asked,
And surely never dreaming that
They do a heavenly task.
They may not pluck no golden harp
But thank the Lord above
For ordinary angels
Who fly on wings of love.

II

General and Narrative Poems

Riches

Tough grasses dug their roots into the hillside,
Clinging on despite the harsh terrain,
Thereby giving anchorage and shelter
To dandelions, also staking claim.

And it was there, at breaking light of morning,
As Dawn awakened dewdrops with a kiss,
I found myself midst molten gold and diamonds,
And rich beyond the dreams of avarice .

Opposites Attract

We're not a bit suited,
I'm plump, you are slim.
Whilst you tipple whisky,
I'll have a pink gin.

You tuck in to steak
"It goes down a treat!"
But have gone "Veggie"
And never eat meat .

You practice karate
The kicks and the chops,
I'd rather flash plastic
In all the best shops.

You're jogging, to strengthen
Your muscles and bones .
I'll settle for choccies
And Miss Bridget Jones.

A splash in the shower
And you are content,
I wallow for hours
With candles and scent.

You're tidy, I'm sloppy
My clothes leave a trail.
You're strong and you're silent,
I holler and wail.

I sigh for the stars,
You prefer telescopes,
You watch all the sport,
I'm hooked on the soaps.

At least there is one thing
On which we agree,
I love you like crazy…
You're nuts about me!

Magic

Come, sit beside me, little one
And snuggle really close,
So I can whisper softly in your ear.
For I've a magic secret
I would like to share with you
Because I hold you
Very, very dear.

You cannot see this magic
Or hold it in your hands,
Nor can you take it out with you to play.
And yet, it's all around you,
Hugging you so tight,
Every single minute
Of the day.

All mummies make this magic,
Daddies do as well.
Aunties, uncles, grandmas, grandpas too.
And 'cos they're very special
And when they're extra good,

Then it's shown to little boys
And girls, like you.

For this is special magic
And it comes from deep inside.
A warm and fuzzy feeling in your tum.
It bubbles all around you
From your head down to your toes
While your heart's a-beating
Like a happy drum.

This magic secret has a name,
It's called "I love you so",
And now… It's yours, forever and a day.
And here's the truly magic part
…It grows and grows and grows
With every little bit
You give away.

It's made of hugs and kisses
And cuddles soft and sweet,
With all your favourite toys
Mixed in as well.
It's full of lovely tasty things to make you big and strong.
And chocolate buttons too
To set the spell.

So, that's the magic secret. I have told you all I know.
And I promise you that every word is true.
But after all that talking I feel a little tired...
So can I have a cuddle, please
...From you?

Fallen Angels

I'm simply surrounded by angels
Most of 'em well past their prime,
And lacking the trappings of glory
Which... well... just dropped off, over time .

There's several with wings which are wonky,
And halos set slightly askew,
While trumpets and harps can only be played
Courtesy strong superglue.

They've entered my life willy nilly,
As giftings from those I hold dear,
Perhaps to mark Christmas or birthday,
Or sometimes to comfort and cheer.

They've travelled the years alongside me,
Sharing the downs and the ups.
Perched along dresser and mantel,
Swinging from rails and from hooks.

Now I'm stuck with each heavenly body
Because at the end of the day,
An angel's an angel forever.
You can't simply chuck 'em away.

So I'll cherish these battle-scarred beings
All flying around and above,
And know myself showered with blessings,
For each one was given with love.

Rebirth

The little soul looked up, and saw
That all was shiny bright,
With interlacing rainbows
Reflecting glorious light.
"Oh no!" it cried. "I've let you down
By coming back so soon.
I only went away in March
And now, it's barely June.
I tried to stay, I really did."
A tear fell from its eye
"I only just got used to life.
I didn't want to die.
I'll go right back and start again
And see what I can do."
But Love said "No, my little one
That path is not for you.
Three times you crossed the threshold,
And each time you have lain
In fear and pain and dark despair,
And three times coldly slain."
The little soul was lifted up

In Love's sublime embrace,
And all its grievous wounds were healed
With tenderness and grace.
It breathed a sigh and snuggled down
As happy as could be,
Then had a little look around…
And looking, it could see
That by a door below, stood souls
In long and winding queue.
"…Oh, pity them, they look so sad.
Please let them stay here too."
"Alas," said Love, "it breaks my heart
But each one must return.
They all have many paths to tread
And many things to learn.
For they are Humankind, and all
Possess, for good or ill
Intellect and conscience
And, best of all, free will.
Yet in their arrogance they spurn
Pure truth for shoddy sham
And many lifetimes may elapse
'Ere they be born a lamb."

Alchemy

Since suns have set
And oceans rolled
Mankind has sought,
So we are told,
For secrets which
Bright stars foretold…
The magic which
Turns base to gold.

Pale sorcerers,
Magicians wise,
Winged wizards who
Traverse the skies,
Are searching for
That precious prize…
But looking through
Unseeing eyes.

When sunbeams warm
The sleeping earth,
And blackbird sings

For all he's worth
To welcome Spring,
Proclaim the birth…
Of beauty, hope,
And joy and mirth.

When gold adorns
Bright shrub and tree,
And buttercups
Grow wild and free,
Spreading far
As eye can see…
That's alchemy
        Enough
                For me.

Beggar-my-Neighbour

In the days of my youth I travelled abroad
In many a foreign clime.
To broaden my mind, at Father's expense.
(Well, that's how 'twas done, at the time.)
One day, I remember, I wandered along,
Feeling despondent and blue,
For funds were quite low, and I had to exist
Till next month's allowance came through.
Oh, I'd money enough for lodgings and food
And to take in historical sights,
But lacked the means of ending the day
'Neath the glitz of the cabaret lights.
Drifting along, not an aim in my head,
I entered a market square ,
Seeing, amongst all the hustle and noise
The beggars a-squatting down there.
Mostly they huddled together in groups,
Just one sat apart and alone…
A string-held placard about her neck,
An ancient and withered old crone.
I sauntered over and stooped down low
To see what the placard said,
And the words thereon smote the door of my heart

For "I'm blind and I'm deaf" it read.
Blind and deaf, alone and old… I looked on the upturned face,
Expecting despair and bitterness there
At the outcome of life's hard race.
Instead, I saw peace and serenity
And marvelled how that could be so
In one who was deaf and blind and lacked
All that the world could bestow.
For, all bound up in the blackness within,
With life left unseen and unheard,
How could she touch the colours of Spring,
Or trace the song of a bird?
Taking the money I'd carried along
('Twas only the price of a meal)
I pressed it deep in the palm of her hand
So that she might feel it was real.
Then I saw that her face held a radiant glow,
Like that of a mystic or seer,
As she basked in some inner light, and swayed
To music which angels can hear.
She reached out then, and took my hand,
Just holding it close for a while,
As a tear rolled down her hollow cheeks
And her lips curved up in a smile.
Then she pressed my hand to those smiling lips
And my heart leaped high in my breast,
Then I left that square, and I walked on air,
In the knowledge that I had been blessed.

Dandelion

Vibrant head of burnished gold
Full of life and brash and bold.
Brighter far than polished gem,
Sunshine on a slender stem.
Wild and wilful, strong and free
Epitomising nature's plea
To human senses, mind and heart,
"Feel the rhythm, be a part
Of all creation's wondrous song.
Nurture, understand, belong.
Grasp life's hand and hold on tight
Grow towards the warmth and light."
Lowly friend of mouse and mole,
Inspiration for the soul...
Whence the wisdom which decreed
You be designated "weed",
And over looked your joy and power
Untamed, dandy lion flower?

The Picture

Just a little picture
In a dark and dingy shop,
Lying in a box beside
A badly chipped old crock.
I longed to quit that murky place
But when this caught my eye
I stood as rooted to the spot
And could not pass it by.
Lifting it with gentle care
My hands began to shake
As though I held some treasure which
Was liable to break.
It can't have graced a gallery
Or anywhere so grand.
For it was born of paint applied
By amateurish hand.
But, oh I had to have it
No matter what the cost
For it wove a bridge of memories
To years used up and lost.
To magic and enchantment

Where a warm and gentle breeze
Played tag with golden sunbeams
As they dappled through the trees
To shine upon a carpet
Of deepest, deepest blue
And spangle all the diamonds
Dropped by the morning dew.
I paid the coins and rescued it
From cockroaches and mice.
And cleaned it up with loving care
My treasure without price.
And every day I fill my soul
With innocence and glee
And I bless that unknown artist
Whoever they may be.
Without whose inner vision
I know never should
Have found the magic doorway, back
To childhood's bluebell wood.

Transition

Oh, such treasures are found
On the merry-go-round
Of dollars and euros and yen.
For the future's bright
      And Jack's all right.
      The markets have risen again.
      Pursuing their goal
      Whilst the Global soul
      Goes begging for falling crumbs.

And the breakers roar
      On the granite shore
            To the beat of Celestial drums...

Racing to win
As the treadmills spin
Creating a silken cocoon.
      Stampede to the top
      Ignoring the drop,
      Like rats to the Piper's tune.
      While shepherds slip
      On an ego trip,
      The sheep have wandered astray.

But grey seals ride
      On the surging tide,
            Which carries the castles away.

Machines do the thinking
Unswerving, unblinking,
Bereft of all doubting or fears.
      Digi-connected,
      Push-button selected,
      Though no-body listens or hears.
      When the end of the day
      Brings a time to pay,
      And the reckoning's mortally high.

Then Innocence grieves
      'Neath the falling leaves
            And weeps with the seabird's cry.

The Binding

Leaning towards me
Your features folded into sympathetic creases
You say, "Lovely to see you. It's been so long.
How is he now?
At the Centre today? Oh that's nice .Gives you
A bit of time for yourself.
We must have coffee together… soon… catch up."
And you mean it sincerely, heading off
Into your parallel universe.
"My Own Time" ticks away
As I fill the supermarket trolley.

With food to prepare
And cook and eat, but never taste.
All purpose cleaner, disinfectant, bleach,
Giant Super Bio. A thank offering
To the Constant Washing Machine.
Four maple muffins. He likes those and
They are not too messy.
Unpack now and put away
Save the plastic bags. They're very handy.
Bring the washing in before it rains.

Now clean the room .
Sweep out. "Why ?". Scrub away. "If only." Just clean…
Ah but, you see, this is not right… not meant to be.
Not part of the Golden Fifty-Year Plan.
To love and to cherish. Yet in this room
Love is daily tempered into duty
To bind the breaking heart.
In sickness and in health.
Till death do us part.
Death wears many disguises.

Nice and clean. Aired. Empty.
Ready to be filled again with
Socks and sleeves and velcro fastenings and
Muscle-cramping, bone-grating, mind-stealing,
Soul-numbing weariness. And yet, withal
Illumined by brief, bright moments…
A look of half-remembering, a name recalled
A belly-laugh. Fingers touching…
Just time for a cup of tea, before they bring him home.
Please God, don't let them be early.

The Ship

One day, in May, I went to play,
As oft I'd done before,
Upon the grassy clifftops
Which overlook the shore.
I flopped upon my belly
And squinted out to sea
And waited for a pirate ship
To show itself to me,
Her crew, they would be cut-throats.
Their captain, Fearsome Fred,
He wore a stripey jumper
And a scarf around his head.
Or p'raps there would be smugglers
In little fishing smacks
With kegs of moonshine whiskey
Under piles of rope and sacks.
I scanned the whole horizon
To see what I could spy
For nothing ever could escape
My telescopic eye.

As scooty clouds played hide and seek
A shaft of brilliant light
Lit up the sea, and oh, I whooped
And shouted with delight.
For there, right there, before me
So wondrous to behold
There sailed a ship, a treasure ship
All made of burnished gold.
And from her ruby funnels
Billowed rosy, pearly smoke
Which spread around about her
Like a lovely, swansdown cloak.
With portholes made of diamonds
And deck of silver gilt
She surely was the fairest
Sailing vessel ever built.
But then the clouds resumed their game
And shuttered out the sun.
My golden ship, she disappeared
Her hour of glory done.

Instead, a weary steamer
With rusty prow and hull
Went about her daily run
Her paint all scratched and dull .
And l was filled with wonder
As I thought of all I'd seen.
I knew it was a miracle
Which never might have been.

For if the sun had not shone out
That very moment when
The rusty ship was chugging by
To catch the light, and then
If I had not been there to see
The marvel of it all...
The moment would have passed, and never
Held me in its thrall.
I've locked the memory in my heart
Inside a secret den,
For when I'm grown , I know that I
May need it now and then.

When days are dark, I'll light them with
That play day by the sea
And reminisce the sun, the ship
The miracle and me.

Rich man, Poor man

When we're poor, we tend to think
That riches pave the way
To happiness, contentment
And sunshine every day.
We see the clothes, the houses,
The yachts, the gems, the cars,
And wish we had the glitter, which
Surrounds these blessed stars.
And there's no doubt, no doubt at all
That money pays the bills,
And keeps out thirst and hunger
And the worst of winter's chills
Riches can enable, open doors
And pave the way,
And put a bit of sunshine
In a dark and rainy day

But, gazing thus, we only see
A fraction of the view,
For billionaires and princes,
They have their heartbreaks too.

For riches, being fickle,
Can leave and not come back.
It only takes a gamble,
Bad judgement or the sack.
Yet, should those gilded pinnacles
Revert to shifting sands.
Wealth untold may still be found
In loving, helping bands.
Though pockets may be empty,
And prospects seem unsure ,
With Gold Reserves of Friendship
Who then could call us poor?

Put out the Stars

Supremacy of intellect
Places Man, it seems
First in all Creation
And architect of dreams.
Doctor, Lawyer, Preacher,
Politician, Engineer.
Pushing back the boundaries
Of ignorance and fear.

> Build it bigger, build it better,
> Build it higher, clear the ground.
> Raze the forest, dig the meadow
> Never pause to look around.
> Keep on moving. Time is money
> What you get is what you earn.
> No commercial value...
> No commission, no return.
> Growth and progress. On-line banking
> Self improvement. Find out how
> You too can make a million
> Have it all and have it now.

Play the markets, make a killing
Buy yourself a brand new face
For it's Devil take the hindmost
When you're in the human race.

Put out the stars, close veil the sun
And make a deal with Death
To stand, unmoved as stone, as earth
Draws slow and laboured breath.
While the fine and wondrous balance
Which embraces sea and land
Is choked and violated by
That intellectual hand.

Transformation

There's a path which leads to nowhere
At the bottom of the lane,
Ending in a patch of common ground.
Where piles of garden rubbish
Find their final resting place,
In ugly, tangled, twisted, withered mound.
Uncared for and untended,
An eye-sore and a dump.
A blot upon the landscape. A disgrace.
No birds, no bees, no butterflies,
No creatures of the field,
No, nothing lived, in that benighted place.

Till nature, taking pity
On the sad, neglected spot,
Called upon her fairies and her sprites
To sprinkle it with magic and
To weave a spell or two,
Filled with joy and wonder and delight.

And there, one sunny morning

I beheld their handiwork,
Fair as any cultivated plot.
Spangled o'er with daisies,
Dipped in dandelion gold,
With, here and there, a shy forget-me-not.
All wrapped round with poppies
And garlanded with light.
A vibrant chord in earth's sublime refrain.
A little bit of Eden, located just beyond
The path which leads to nowhere,
At the bottom of the lane.

Chimes

Someone half a world away
In soft and sunny clime
Took twine, bamboo and coco shell
And made of them a chime
They listened to the mellow notes
Made sure that they rang true
Then put a little blessing in
The heart of the bamboo.
Sent them on a journey
Their destiny to be
Sold and bought and sold again
And gifted, then, to me.
To grace an English garden
And catch an English breeze.
And serenade the growing shoots
Of cabbages and peas.
And nightly, 'neath a starbright sky
By gently lapping sea
Sway with a velvet rhythm
And softly sing to me
A ballad of that far-off land
As sweet as heady wine
The music of the spirit
Of the hand that held the twine.

It's Mrs Tommy Johnson, God...

It's Mrs Tommy Johnson, God,
Come knocking at your door.
I know you haven't seen me, much
Around this way before.
I've never prayed an awful lot,
Just never felt the need.
Don't understand that Holy stuff
With candles, choir and creed.
But now I'm sitting, lonely
In the deepness of the night,
I need to hold to Something
Or to Someone, very tight.
For I mustn't go to pieces
There's the kids to think about,
And tell them Daddy's coming home
Oh yes... sure thing... no doubt.
I don't know when, exactly
But it's bound to be quite soon,
And then he'll make us laugh again,
The great big, soft buffoon.
That's just how we'll think of him,

That's what they'll understand.
…Not lying, smashed to pieces
On the hot and bloodied sand…

Oh God! I cannot bear it…
But I've got to. There's no choice,
So, if somebody's out there, and
If you can hear my voice,
My thoughts are all a jumble.
And I don't know where to start
Please… Oh, will you listen
'Cos I'm speaking with my heart.
My Tommy, Sergeant Johnson,
Please keep him safe and well,
For I love him, see, I love him
More'n words can ever tell.
And even, s'pose he's wounded,
Well, that's all right, for then
We'd soon all be together
So's to love him well again.
But if… I daresn't say it
For fear it may come true…
Though I know I've got to face it.
As others have to do.
So, if he's called to give his life
Please… spare his agony.
Father, in your kindness,
Just set his spirit free.
And in his final moments

When all is calm and still,
Please, let him know we love him
…Let him know we always will.
Well, God, I'm going to finish now.
You've got enough to do.
I s'pose they're queuing round the world
All trying to get through…
They may speak another language
Call you by a different name,
But love transcends all boundaries,
Please…
      God…
            Bring him home again.

The Almighty Dollar

Gee, that was tough, a really close call
And it's taken me most of the day.
But oysters and steak and a bottle of Rye
Kinda helped him to see things my way.
Now it's almost five and she'll skin me alive
I said I'd be home by two
But a deal's a deal and a buck's a buck
So what's a fella to do?
I promised I'd help with Joe's party you see.
And boy, am I long overdue...
Now Carrie, she'll cry and swear I don't care
And I guess that we'll fight, but what's new?
Gee it's no big deal, if she'd cut the spiel.
She would have to admit, if she's fair
The kid was too busy with candy and cake
To notice that I wasn't there.
She's got to get her priorities right
Gotta see things my way.
Guess I'll rest here for a minute or two
It's been one helluva day.
Maybe I'll take me a ten-minute nap

Under this maple tree
Well... Hi, old man, where'd you come from?
Sure... come and sit by me.

      Who are you, old man? For you seem to be changed
      And your face bas grown bright as the sun
      There's something about you that fills me with dread
      And I can't seem to move, or I'd run.
      You bid me be silent and listen and learn
      And it's then that I hear you say
      "Your wealth is not measured by what you have got
      But by all that you've given away.
      No matter how hard or how high you may climb,
      No matter how loud is your song,
      Success is not beating them all to the line
      But helping the others along.
      In time, my son, we must meet again
      In a different, distant land
      When the play is done and the race is run
      Then you will understand
      How dark is life's path, with its twists and its turns
      And how, at the end of the day,
      A flame of love in the heart and the soul
      Is all that can light up the way."
Wow... what a dream... Say... was it a dream?
Already it's starting to fade
Well I guess someday I may figure it out
But for now... there are deals to be made.

Lost

Where did all the memories go?
Once so I bright and clear,
Stored against a rainy day
To comfort, bind and cheer.
I don't know when they slipped away
Nor why, nor how they went,
And left me here. Alone. Adrift,
My compass needle bent.

I thought I'd always have them
As a part of being me,
Like childhood's summer castles
And autumn's russet tree.
But years and tides have washed away
Those turrets in the sand.
And trees, beset by winter winds
Now knarled and naked stand.

And stretching back, behind me
A winding path is there
With footprints chasing fleeting time

All leading back to... where?
What brought me to this empty place?
Why must I stand alone,
No wish to stay, no will to move
My heart a lumpen stone.

Have I known light and laughter?
And sometimes, were there tears?
Did someone take my hand, in love
And share the passing years?
And what of all the songs we sang
And all the words we said?
Where have all the memories gone?
...They're not inside my head.

Jenny's tea

Hello dear, can you help me? I must get to the shops.
This door, it won't come open. I think, perhaps, it's locked.
Albert needs his dinner.
I know he'd like a stew
What's that dear…? In a minute…
Come and sit with you?
Well, only for a moment
I'm in a rush, you see.
'Cause I can't do my shopping
'Till I've made Jenny's tea.
Oh my, what lovely flowers
No! Really? They're for me?
I'll put them in a vase as soon
As I've got Jenny's tea.
Have you seen my Jenny?
She can't be far away
I'd better go and find her;
She's just gone out to play.
What's that, dear? You're my Jenny
Oh no. That can't be so.
She's only eight, with gappy teeth

And hair tied in a bow.
There, there, love, don't be crying
Oh, what has made you sad?
Come on, let's have a smile now
It can't be all that bad.
But have you seen my Jenny?
She's in her new pink dress.
Her daddy bought it yesterday
He calls her his princess.
You're going now dear, are you?
Back in a day or two.
Well, it's been nice to meet you…
I think I'll do a stew.
He loves a stew, does Albert
He'd eat it fit to burst
I'll maybe make some dumplings, but
I must find Jenny first.
You've got a lovely smile, dear
Reminds me of… let's see…
Whatever was I going to do?
Oh yes… get Jenny's tea.

Communion

I met a man, the other day,
Who told me that he did not pray.
Yet every evening he toiled late,
Preparing food, so he could wait
On hungry, homeless, hopeless folk.
And though 'tis true, he never spoke,
A formal word of praise or prayer,
I saw his soul was praying there.

Feed the birds...

Scattered trail of breadcrumbs
All mixed up with seeds,
Sparrows picking, pecking
Follow where it leads.
Watch her walking slowly
Tho' the skies be grey,
There's no need to hurry.
High spot of the day.
Sitting on a bench now
'Neath a chestnut tree,
A waiting, willing captive
With manna for the free.
Every day she comes here,
Be it fine or wet,
Will not leave them hungry,
Never failed them yet.
This the point of contact,
This is where they meet,
Giving and receiving.
Circle is complete.
Fluttering to meet her,
Coaxing out a smile,
All the lonely living
Put on hold a while.

"Mistical" Morn

A magical, "mistical" day has begun.
Earth stirs from slumber. Riverlets run
Calling to cobwebs, all spidery spun
With transient diamonds kissed by the sun.

Tick Tock

Today I heard the ticking of the clock.
It seemed to come from somewhere very near.
Marking off the minutes and the hours,
Impassive and unstoppable and clear.
Reminding me of passing days and years,
Of cosmic ebb and flow and rise and fall,
And how time, though as infinite as space,
Serves portions which are very, very small.
Each second, packaged there, is running wild,
Forever free, beguiling and untamed.
Precious, fleeting particles of light.
And none, once spent, can ever be reclaimed.

Transformation

I spied the leaf upon the wood,
Saw the river surge and flood,
Felt the binding ties of blood,
Watched the ocean... understood
The here and there, the now and then
Carved in stone or scribed by pen
And held within the minds of men,
The hallelujah and amen.
Saw summers aye give way to frost,
And vessels sorely tempest toss't
And Life evolve despite the cost,
With nothing wasted, nothing lost.
I saw, beneath eternal skies,
Though all things change, yet nothing dies,
But, weaving rainbow cosmic ties
Lives on again, in other guise.

Delight

Tiny creature of feather and wing,
How many times have I heard you sing?
And felt my in-most self imbued
With awe, delight and gratitude.
As crystal notes filled pre-dawn air
With healing, hope and praise and prayer.
How many times have I watched unfold
The saffron and rose and crimson and gold
Of morning's glory spreading high,
Across an arched, expansive sky.
Spring-time's, blossom-dappled days,
Summer's rosy-scented haze,
Winter's diamonds, autumn's gold,
Transient gifts of joy untold.
How oft? It matters not at all.
Such pure delights can never pall.
They are, like softly settled dew,
Always fresh and ever new.

Giving Thanks

I am grateful for

> Each day's package of unopened time,
> Minutes, seconds, hours...
> Gift-wrapped in hopes and possibilities.

And for

> The soft footfalls of evening,
> Ushering in dark, star-crowned night,
> Bearing restoration and repose.

And for

> The seasons of the year,
> Riding their rainbow carousel.
> Springtime and harvest and silver and gold.

And for

> The lessons of today, and the hopes of tomorrow,
> The strength of friendship, the consolation of solitude.
> Love, in all its colours, shapes and sizes.

And for

> Sustenance for bodies and manna for souls,
> The light of understanding and the comfort of compassion
> And for the existence of angels.

Spirals

Once upon a time
    Love ignited,
    Hearts delighted,
    Wrongs were righted.
    And all was wonderful
        And sunlight-kissed and fair.

'Twas just a mime,
    Time turned the tide,
    Spring sickened, died.
    Nowhere to hide.
    And all was cold
        And no-one seemed to care.

Yet hope's sublime,
    Tho' life may crash
    Within the ash
    A tiny flash
    Illuminates
        A phoenix there.

War And Peace

The old soldier remembers...

They're marching past the cenotaph,
They're standing tall and straight.
They're laying wreaths of poppies
And they're preaching love, not hate.

Oh tell 'em Padre, tell 'em
As war's not worth the toss.
There never aint no victories
Just loss, just bloody loss.

It's more than sixty years ago
Since I went off to fight.
Old Fritz... he needed teaching,
Well, we'd stitch him up, right tight.

'Twould only take a month or so.
We'd show him what was what,
Then all come home as heroes
Wearing medals, like as not.

Them months stretched into years and years.

Oh tell 'em Padre, tell
How "Marching to Adventure"
Became a crawl through hell.

One day… p'raps it were yesterday…
It seems that way, you see…
We came upon the enemy
As near as you to me.

I opened fire… I had no choice,
But firing, I could see
Inside that German unifom
Were… just a lad… like me.

And as my bullets hit him
I could hear… it weren't that far,
How, in his dying agony
He screamed out… for his Ma…

And there and then I knew the truth
As clear as clear could be
How I'd just killed my brother,
I were him… and he were me.

No! I don't need no poppies
My memories never cease
They're graven on my very soul…
For me, there is no Peace.

Courage...

You may feel that you can touch it
As it crackles in the air,
Or see it wearing gaudy robes
With style, panache and flair.
And hear it shouting boldly,
"To the devil with all care."
Or you may just catch a whisper,
"I can, I will, I dare."

It may take the lead in battle,
Causing mayhem in the fray,
Or ride out, killing dragons
'Till there's no more left to slay.
Or blaze a trail through danger
Showing other folk the way.
Or struggle out of bed, to face
Another pain-filled day.

It can't be purchased, nor is it
Within one's gift to give.
It has been known to drain away

Like water through a sieve.
Oft needed to admit to wrong
And always to forgive.
Some call on it when facing death,
And others just to live.

Pictures

I'm not quite sure what day it is
Or what year, come to that.
Did I put the kettle on?
And have I fed the cat?
My memory's not what it was...
The rest of me is fair,
But, with the mileage on the clock
There must be rust somewhere!
You ask "Who is prime minister?"
"Have we a queen or king?"
...I just plain don't remember
No... not a blessed thing!
They say that it's an illness
Though I don't feel all that sick
Not when I think of Blackpool
And the pier and "Kiss me Quick."
In fact, I feel quite chipper
Fine and dandy, full of pluck
It's just this modern living
As makes me come unstuck.

      I remember going fishing
      With bent-up pins for hooks.
      I remember air-raid shelters
      Gas masks and ration books.

And I remember summers
That were wide as they were long
Full of streams and meadows
And hay-making and song.
I remember thinking babies
Were flown in by the stork
I remember toasting teacakes
On a four-pronged toasting fork,
Lying on the hearthrug
As the fire glowed red and blue
While Dad told great tall stories
And swore each one was true.
"Look hard," he'd say, "and see them…
The fairies in the fire,"
And the flames, why they were dancers
Leaping higher, ever higher.
We didn't have much money
But then, we didn't care
We had our mam, we had our dad
We had the pictures there.
Now, I can't do with computers
And I seldom watch TV.
The wireless, that's my favourite
For it keeps me company
As I sit here in my time warp
With my laughter and my tears
And remember all the living
And the loving through the years.
I visualize the faces
And call to mind the names
As I watch them all a-dancin'
With the fairies, in the flames.

Seedlings

A tiny spark may start a conflagration.
That constant drip will wear away a stone,
And spreading oaks can spring from little acorns,
And babes may light and lead the world, once grown.
One silver note awakes Dawn's feathered songsters,
A single word gives birth to mighty tomes.
All journeyings must follow on from one initial step,
And minutes, seconds, hours, are simply clones.
Nothing just appears as though by magical decree.
From small beginnings all things make a start.
Faith can move a mountain. Hope can reach the stars,
And a little bit of love can mend a heart.

Who Made the Music?

Who made the music?
Who played a part
In lifting the mind
And easing the heart.
Who played the notes
So old yet so new
Vibrant as raindrops
Soft as the dew.
Who heard the tune
In that great otherwhere
And wrote down the score
So that others might share.
Who strung the bow
Whose consumate skill
Gave it the power
To soothe and to thrill.
Who carved the wood
Whose hand held the knife
Transforming with love
And bringing to life.

Who's the creation
Who set it free
Who made the music
Who made the tree?

Questions

Why can't it last forever,
Why must we weaken and die?
Why can't we stay together,
Why can't we learn how to fly?

Why must the brave and mighty fail,
And the shining be eaten by rust?
Why do the winds tear a hole in the sail
And the mountains all crumble to dust?

Why must the blossoms wither and fade,
And clouds hide the face of the moon?
Why are the banners all tattered and frayed?
Why must it end so soon?

The answer comes soft, with the rustle of leaves,
In the seasonal song which they sing.
Through summer and autumn and winter, time weaves
The advent and rebirth of spring.

Perfect Recall

Many and many the years which have washed
Under the bridges of time,
Bearing the love which I held in my heart
And all the devotion in thine.
Yet leaving behind, at the sundering hour,
A memory, bitterly sweet.
Captured for aye in that ultimate sigh
Where living and dying must meet.

For you left, you left, in youth's soft arms
In spite of entreaties to stay.
Whilst I remain, in this lesser-lit world,
To see out the rest of the play.
And when the curtain at last comes down,
And it's time to remove all disguise,
Will I still be as you saw me last,
And beautiful, love, in your eyes?

Snoozin'

Little tabby pussy cat
Lying in the sun,
Gently, gently toasting,
Till one side is done.
Languidly roll over,
Rearrange a paw,
Flitter ears and whiskers,
Go to sleep once more.
Deeply, deeply slumber,
Wrapped in feline dream
Of fishy things and catnip mice
And saucers full of cream.
Let no care disturb you,
Know, whate'er you crave
Will be laid before you,
By your willing slave.
Epitome of furry grace,
Embodiment of fun,
Little tabby pussy cat
Lying in the sun.

Don't Blame Poor Old Money.

I've heard it said that money is the root of all that's bad.
I'm not sure I agree with that. I think it's rather sad
To label poor old money, and give 'im a bad name,
For you cannot blame the dice, my friend, it's how you play the game
Of course, you 'ave to teach 'im just how he must behave.
You 'ave to be the master, else you will be his slave.
The trick is having just enough – too much can make you tight
And not enough is worrisome, but just enough is right.
He puts warm clothes upon the back and shoes upon the feet.
He lights the fire and pays the bills and buys a bite to eat.
He likes to have a bit of fun and dress up to the nines.
He'll always try to help a friend what's fallen on hard times.
At Christmas time, why then, he hangs a present on the tree.
So, money, he aint doin' bad, as far as I can see.
He's like some poor foot soldier, as could be me or you,
Sent by them bloomin' generals, to do what he must do.
That doesn't mean he likes it, or thinks it's okay doke.
He has to go where he is sent; he's got no choice, poor bloke.
Sometimes the fight is dirty and the cause aint all that just
But he just has to do it… It's orders, see… he must.
But he'd rather be the good guy, buildin' bridges, carting wheat,
An' giving folks a helping hand to get back on their feet.
Clearing up the damage, putting right the wrong,

So as little kiddies can grow up tall and strong.
So, don't blame poor old money, it's crystal clear to see
The fault don't lie with him at all, it sits with you and me.
If each of us just does our best and treats him right and kind.
Well, we won't feel so bad, that day, when we leave him behind,
And rich or poor won't matter then, tycoon or on the dole,
When the colour of our money is reflected in our soul.

Shifting shape

I used to think a pyramid
Explained the way things are,
With mankind ranged around the base
And at the top, a star.
And every day, in every way
We'd struggle to ascend,
Advancing slowly, inch by inch,
And hoping, in the end
By means of goodly thoughts and deeds
To find a little spot
That's near to saints and angels, and
Away from all that's hot.

But now, you know, I fancy that
I got it very wrong,
Imagining us far away
From Heaven's shining throng.
Instead, I'm sure the whole of Life
Is close, as close can be,
Everything that's visible
And all we cannot see.

From where I'm standing now, there's not
A pyramid in sight,
Instead I see a circle,
And it's filled with love and light.

There is no separation
As all creation stands
Side by side together,
Reaching out and holding hands.

III

Humorous

Age before beauty

I don't know which forces have brought me
Right here and right now to this place.
I'm not even sure it is me anymore,
That certainly isn't my face!
I used to be frilly and girly,
Well known for my charm and my flair.
But now I'm all jumpers and wellies,
And a "Don't mess with me!" kind of glare.
What brought on this metamorphosis,
Turning me into a drudge?
Who stole the wine and the roses?
Somebody find me a Judge.
I'm suing for full restitution,
I'll take compensation as well,
And why should I stop at half measures
…Throw in a magical spell.
So that's it, I'll bathe in youth's fountain,
And turn back those silly old clocks
I'll dust off my pointy stilettos
And wear flouncy tight-waisted frocks.
So bye bye to baggy old comfort,
And welcome back hold-the-breath glam,
No… hang on, I've just found my marbles
…I reckon I'll stay as I am!

Overtaken

Technology's leaving me stranded,
Progress is passing me by.
I'm relegated to yesteryear,
Not knowing the "how" or the "why".
I'm quite au fait with the telephone…
LANDLINE, I hasten to add,
For a "mobile" has me all fingers and thumbs,
I know, I know, ain't it sad!
I can cope with the kettle, the toaster's a breeze
And the pressure cooker's OK
The microwave though, I secretly fear
Might well run amok one day.
I'm on good terms with the washing machine,
Show me an iron… I'm cool,
The tele's a friend, but that video thing
Can make me appear quite a fool.
And PCs and laptops and aught of that ilk
Just leave me a quivering wreck,
I'm quite convinced they have minds of their own…
And how do you keep them in check?
I'd never dare to switch one on,

I wouldn't be so rash.
I know that they may go awry,
I've heard that things can crash.
And should I chance to touch a key,
...This really makes me fret...
I fear that I might punch a hole
Right through that internet.
So, I'll just give the high-tech stuff
A nod, and e'en a wink,
And continue to write letters
On paper, and with ink.
Let others use the fast lane,
I wish them all "God's Speed".
I'll settle down in "Fogeyland"
And simply go to seed.

No Contest

I've got lotions, I've got creams
With the magic power, it seems
To banish lines and wrinkles, by and bye.
And with shades of every hue
I'll do what I must do
To embellish skin and lip and cheek and eye.
Then... In an hour or three
Why, daisy-fresh I'll be...
       But daisies do not even have to try!

I've top designer labels,
Slinky jodhpurs for the stables.
Whilst I snuggle into cashmere when I'm cold.
And with each accessory
Being so completely "me"
I'm a vision of perfection, so I'm told.
But I'm under no illusion
For "perfection"... see the fusion
       Of sunset's pink and red and molten gold.

I've perfume and cologne,
From "discreet" to "overblown",
Which tantalize the senses through the nose.
With bubbly bathtime stuff,
Dusting powder on a puff,
I'm aroma'd from my head down to my toes.
But I must admit defeat
For I simply can't compete
      With a sweetly scented, wildly rambling rose.

I have necklaces and rings
And all sorts of pretty things
Inlaid with gems and diamonds from afar.
My strings of perfect pearls
Are the envy of the girls.
My collection would do credit to a tsar.
But it's such an awful waste,
They might just as well be paste
      For not one can hold a candle to a star.

Holiday Postcard

Just a line
From lovely… (wow
What is this place,
Where are we now?)

Journey was smooth
Got here OK
(Discounting the fog
And the ten-hour delay).

There's so much to do
And so much to see.
(And I'd kill to sit down
With a nice cup of tea).

Weather is sunny and
Warm, in the main
(They say 'twas a freak
That old hurricane).

The natives are all
Wearing national dress
(The daggers are part of
The costume, I guess).

Swimming is great
If you dare to go in
(But keep well away from
That diamond-shaped fin).

Food is delicious
The portions are great
(I'm sure it's a bug
Not something I ate).

Hoping to come back
Refreshed and reborn
(Next year we're having
A tent on the lawn).

Rise above it...

I sometimes find it very hard
To practice what I preach,
And rise above life's wrongs and hurts
As all the good books teach.

'Tis hard, when you are being mugged
By some pugnacious lout
Not to wish a lightning bolt
Would come and sort him out.
Hard not to hope, when someone's conned
Your precious, hard-earned cash,
That be will meet a cannibal
Who'll turn him into hash!
When thieves break in and loot and steal
And vandalise your house,
It's hard to keep from wishing
You could squash 'em, like a louse.

But, hey, I'll try, I really will,
I'll strive to understand
What drives the troubled, twisted mind,

What prompts the thieving hand
I'll pray for their immortal souls.
I'll make the heavens ring,
And doing so, perhaps I'll grow
A feather for my wing!

Healthy Eating

I'm in the supermarket, with my trolley, set to go,
And in my hand, a list, so that I'll absolutely know
What to buy... The things I can't... And all the things I can,
To start me on my new regime. My healthy eating plan.
All set then... lots of veggies, carrots, beans, and cauliflowers...
Oh, but just a minute now, it's going to take me hours
Of scrubbing, peeling, chopping. I'll be worn out, on my knees.
Perhaps, for the time being, I'll just take these frozen peas.
Lettuce and tomatoes, for those balmy salad days.
A great big tub of coleslaw and a jar of mayonnaise.
Milk that's skimmed, the leanest ham, and here's some low-fat cheese,
With French bread and some pickles – I could make a meal of these.
Pasta now, that's very good. Wholewheat's best, they say.
Except that when I cook it, it resembles sticky clay,
And coaxing it out of the pan takes quite a bit of force,
Oh! Here's some in a "Ready Meal", with lots of lovely sauce.
Water, crispbread, fruit and oats... I know I'm going to win,
But, just to bolster my resolve, I'd better take some gin.
Oooh, look at that Pavlova! Oh isn't it a dream!

Meringue and luscious raspberries, and all filled up with cream.
I mustn't... No... I shouldn't... oh all right then... I give in,
I'm only human. Surely I'm allowed one tiny sin?
Well, it's taken simply ages... Oh no! Look at the time!
Still... it's been worth each minute, for soon I'll feel divine.
Just look at all that healthy stuff. It makes you smack your lips
Too late now, to cook it though. I'll just get fish and chips.

Cobwebs

A cobweb is a spider's home
But, domicile apart,
It is a thing of beauty and,
A wondrous work of art.
Hanging from a trellis fence
Or bush or branch or wall,
Oft used by elves and fairies
At dawning, as they trawl
The dewy grass for diamonds
Kissed by the rising sun,
And lit with rainbow colours
Playing hide-and-seek for fun.
A finishing of fairy dust
To set the magic free,
And everything is ready then
For humankind to see.

I don't know how the spider feels
About this elfin sport.
Will he sue for damages
In some arachnid court?

Or is he really quite relaxed,
Not one for fight or feud,
Content to let things be, and just
Become a Diamond Dude?
So, knowing that enchantment
Is in very short supply…
When I see cobwebs in the house
I simply pass them by…
Hoping that the little folk
Will weave a magic spell
And turn my darkest comers
Into fairy lands as well.

The Rummage Sale

Oh good, they've opened up on time,
And we're first through the door.
My dear, I simply can't believe
You've not "done one" before!
They're really all the rage, you know,
Addictive, I'll confess,
But better far than yoga
For alleviating stress.
Let's rummage through the bric-a-brac
The good stuff goes so quick,
They're like a plague of locusts.
It really makes one sick
The way that people push and shove,
Oh look... there... can you see...
That box of "bits" looks tempting.
Quick, give them all to me,
And grab that pretty bracelet
There now... what do you think?
Oh, I wouldn't say it's broken,
No... there's just a missing link.
Now don't go looking down your nose
And wrinkling up your brow,
You have to understand, my dear
You're not in Harrod's now!

Dash to the clothes.
That blouse is nice.
I'd wear it, at a pinch.
Now, wedge yourself beside me here
And don't give way an inch.
Oh, see that lovely, pleated skirt,
The colours are divine.
No... no... gerroff... I saw it first,
Let go, I say... It's mine!
That showed her! What? Not ladylike?
Well... true... (though one recoils)...
It's rather like a combat sport.
The victor takes the spoils.
What? It's a ten and I'm a twelve,
That matters not a bit.
I'll let it out on all the seams,
'Twill be a perfect fit.
Dresses, jumpers, scarves and gloves,
Just stuff them in the sack.
I'll check them in a minute, and
Then throw the duff stuff back
C'mon, let's go. Is that your lot?
You've missed the boat, I fear.
What's that? You cannot see the point?
I'll try to make it clear.
Look... Here's the prize I bagged today,
I'll lay it on this table.
Well yes, it's old and frayed and worn,
But, darling... see THE LABEL!

Time – less

I don't have the time to be tired.
I haven't the space for a slump.
Those persons genteelly exhausted...
Well frankly, they give me the hump.
OK, I'll admit it. I'm jealous,
I'd like to be fragile and wan.
But I'm just a stuck ugly duckling
Who's never turned into a swan.
I haven't a moment for moaning,
The chores are all jostling in queues.
I'm trying to keep them in order
By issuing signed IOUs.
I'd really like someone to gift me
An extra twelve hours in each day,
Wrapped up in ribbon and brought by
The man in the ads for Milk Tray!
I can't see the work dissipating
Or even abating a smidge,
Perhaps I will simply swap brushes
And go off and paint the Forth Bridge.
But hey, I've a dream, an ambition,
Long standing and heartfelt and deep,
To treat myself to a vacation
...And spend the whole fortnight asleep.

The Queue

I'm standing in a queue
And ahead there's quite a few
Trolleys, which are piled up to the brim.
Now we're stuck here, nose to tail
In this Supermarket jail,
And chances of release are looking slim.

The girl behind the till
Has completely lost the will
To scan the bar-codes with the speed of light.
In fact, right now it seems
She is sinking into dreams…
And she isn't even putting up a fight.

My empty stomach rumbles,
And creaks and groans and grumbles,
And slow starvation may well be my fate.
Would it make an awful racket
If I opened up a packet
And crunched a crisp before it is too late?

At last! A chink of blue
For someone's just gone through,
And I feel like shouting hip-hip-hip hooray!
Hang on… We've hit a snag
For she cannot find her bag,
It's come as quite a shock she has to pay!

Control begins to slip
As I start to lose my grip
And trolley rage is looking set to pounce,
When a sudden little thought
Somehow pulls me up quite short
And lifts my heart, and makes it skip and bounce.

I feel a surge of glee.
It's OK, being me,
I have no cause to grumble at my lot.
I can hear and see and talk,
I can touch and feel and walk,
And there's oh-so-many others who cannot.

Who would love to join this queue,
To live as others do,
So… 'ere that red mist rages round my head ,
I'll stop champing at the bit,
Leave my so-short fuse unlit
And simply count my blessings now instead.

Other People's Plates

I'm eating out. My food arrives
I'm tucking in... and drat...
Another plate is wafted by...
...I wish I'd ordered that.

And look, a great big bowl piled high
With chips both long and fat.
My hips might not agree, but oh
I wish I'd ordered that.

And there's a fish so large I could
Have saved some for the cat.
Sorry puss, I didn't think.
I wish I'd ordered that.

Steaks and salads, pasta, pies
Crab or squid or sprat,
When laid upon another's plate,
I'll wish I'd ordered that.

And should a platter, borne aloft
Display my only hat,
What's the betting I'd still moan…
I wish I'd ordered that!

Hide and Seek

Everything is growing legs
And playing hide and seek.
It seems to happen every day
And week on bloomin' week .

The purse which I had right to hand
Has upped and done a bunk,
So plans for retail therapy
Are well and truly sunk.

I've got my coat and scarf and gloves,
But now it's "Hunt the Hat".
(And where's that tin of Superchunks
I'd opened for the cat?)

I'm sure I would be better off
Residing in a cave,
For guess who's found the scrubbing brush
Tucked in the microwave?

Not long ago, my pooch and I
Went out to have a jog.
Now here's the lead safe in my hand
But where on earth's the dog?

But hey, there is a brighter side,
I find no cause to grouse,
For all this running up the stairs
And round and round the house,

Is but a blessing in disguise
(I do not jest or jape),
For though the memory's caput,
The rest of me's in shape!

IV

Comfort

Love Survives

Love survives
      Lives on and grows
It gilds the dawn
      And paints the rose.
Soars with birdsong
      Leaps in rain
Graces laughter
      Eases pain.
It lights the soul
      Through countless lives.
All else must fail
      But love survives.

Don't Weep for Me

Don't weep for me, for it was time
To slip life's bonds and soar and climb
To brighter realms, well known before,
Where all is light and love is law.
Do not grieve for what is past,
For bodies are not made to last.
Expendable. Their only role
A growing medium for the soul.
Don't store my books, don't wear my rings
Or cling to clothes or other things
Of sentimental value for
You do not need them anymore.
Browse through photos for a while,
But only if they make you smile
And call to mind how much we cared,
The things we did, the times we shared.
But do not sigh and wish them back
Or dress yourself in hopeless black,
For clouds will part and lark will rise
The wheel must turn, to make us wise.
And this is how 'twill ever be

I'm part of you, you're part of me.
At every dawnings golden flare,
Each velvet nightfall, I'll be there.
On woodland walk, by tossing sea
Some elemental part of me
Will ride the wind and sing it's song
For each to each we all belong.
Your happiness will set me free.
Beloved, do not weep for me.

Time

There is a time, a little time
For every soul to bide,
To blossom and bear fruit, and then
To catch the ebbing tide.

A time to slip life's leaden chains
And, with the wind set fair,
Make sail to blest remembered shores,
And walk with angels there.

Circles

I know that day must follow night
As night must follow day.
And life and death must walk entwined
Along the shadowed way.

This truth brings comfort,
Hope and strength
When all is bleak and stark.
And courage then, to strive to touch
The light beyond the dark.

Not Just Today

Not just today, but every day
'Ere lips can speak or heart can pray.
In light and dark and day and night
Through time and space... I'm woven tight
Within the fabric of your soul
Alive and perfect, healed and whole.
In far off land, by garden plot
Awake, asleep, it matters not.
Secure, within, and there to stay,
Not just today, but every day.

Family

"Dust to dust," The preacher said,
"Ashes to ashes return."
As our grief filled up that hungry grave,
Wreathed in flowers and fern.
Sombre, he raised his hands aloft,
Inviting us all to pray
"We bring nothing into this world," he said,
"We surely take nothing away."
And then it was that I lifted my head
Silent, I drew apart,
Knowing, somehow, that those words were false,
Sure in the depths of my heart.

For your spirit came down all laden with gifts,
Came just to sojurn a while,
Blessing our lives with your wonderful love,
Warming us through with your smile,
Easing and smoothing the pathway of life,
Calming our doubts and our fears.
Leading the way, with your luminous light,
Drying the bitterest tears.

And now... and now... as we bid you farewell,
We know, as your wings unfold
They glow with eternal, rainbow hues
More precious than silver or gold.
And your soul, at the end of this journey
Weighs more than it did at the start,
Wrapped as it is, in the gilding love
Of many and many a heart.
For, all that we bring and take and leave
Lies hidden from mortal eye,
Minted as coin of the spirit,
Never to wither or die.

Don't ask me to stay...

Don't ask me to stay, with pleading and tears
Binding me tight with your pain
To the weight of all our togetherness years.
You are holding my heart, but in vain.

For, oh, I have glimpsed such a wonderful light,
Shining around and above,
Putting all doubting and anguish to flight.
Glowing with infinite love.

And I feel that arms are opening wide
In welcoming, tender embrace,
As I step from the surf of a slow, ebbing tide
To a dear and remembered place.

Of music and laughter and joy and delight.
Beloved, if you could but see
How everything's made of that luminous light
And all is a part of me,

Why, then you would know, and would understand
That I'm crossing from night into day.
And you'd give me your blessing and hold to my hand,
But you never would ask me to stay.

Tough Love

You, who now are bent and bowed by grief,
Mourning for a love that is no more,
Feeling in each beat of your sad heart
The wounds of chill bereavement's talloned claw.

And those who have not felt Death's dreaded touch,
Yet stand forsaken and alone and cold,
Betrayed and broken-hearted, scarred and maimed
With no one now to call their own or hold.

You feel a dark despair, you're only human,
Your tunnel has no light, no paths, no choice.
But in the stillness there will come a whisper
Murmuring... "Rejoice... rejoice... rejoice."

For if your love had never sought and found you,
To fill your life with warmth and joy and light,
You would not now be stricken and afflicted...
But neither would your soul have taken flight.

Although the storm, at present, rages round you,
Look hard, and see the rainbow through the rain.
Devotion, for a time, lit all your being,
And such a love... is it not worth the pain?

Praying

Oh how I prayed,
My prayers so deep
They'd reach to the ocean bed.
Whilst anguished entreaties
And bargaining pleas
Filled up my heart and my head.

As the fear of your loss
Cut into my soul
Sharper than dagger or knife,
Through hope and despair
And sheer disbelief
I prayed and prayed for your life.

But all was in vain
For the light grew dim
As your brightness ebbed slowly away.
Once more I sought
The Creator's face,
For still, it seemed, I must pray.

"Why?" I cried,
But e'en as I asked,
Somehow, I already knew
That God was in need
Of an angel just then,
And only the brightest would do.

Reunion

All that I have is a photograph.
That, and a lock of your hair,
In a world that is bleak and colourless now
That you are not there… are not there…
And the weight of my loss is dragging me down
'Neath a tidal surging of grief,
For joy and hope are stolen away
By a dread and invincible thief.

Time cannot heal the tear in my heart,
Tears bring no balm as they flow.
There's nothing I'm wanting to do, any more,
And nowhere I'm wishing to go.
Though Earth may be turning as ever she did,
And seasons still sing their refrain,
It is, to me but an empty round
Of yearning despair and of pain.

Yet somehow I know that the essence of you.
That spark of eternal flame,
Is still aglow in the vast unknown ,

And life's but a mirage, a game.
And that being so, then a time must come
As playthings are all put away,
When our souls will unite in eternity's arms,
To walk, in the light, on the way.

Crossing The Void

There is a bridge which spans untold dimensions,
'Tis woven of the love within the heart.
Spun throughout the living of a lifetime,
That souls may ne'er be sundered and apart.

It rises out of swirling mists of longing,
And, strong enough to bear all grief and pain,
Bears travellers across the darkest chasms
To join with all those dearly loved again.

For mind and soul traverse all mortal confines
To dwell within Eternity unbound.
Reality expands to new horizons,
And all that once was lost can now be found

Take but one step see, here's a star to guide you.
Be not afraid, this bridge is very real.
'Twill take you out of black, despairing darkness
Into that light, where broken hearts may heal.

Love Never Goes Away

How could you think I would leave you?
Leave you and shatter your heart.
My spirit adrift in the ether,
Separate. Ever apart.

As gold tips the eastern horizon,
And songbirds entrance a new day,
Great breakers roll in to the shingle
And sea birds dive down through the spray.
While spring decks branches in blossom
And summer warms earth with her glow,
Then autumn gilds cornfield and forest
And winter casts spangles on snow.
Whilst moon and stars light the heavens
And half of the world is asleep,
When loneliness cries out for comfort
And even the soul wants to weep.

Just reach out… you'll find me beside you,
Whenever you call, I will hear.
For love cannot leave the beloved.
I'm near… as a heartbeat is near.

Becoming One

The world was filled with pain and devastation
The day you left me, left me quite alone.
You fled, with death's dark cloak wrapped round about you,
And turned my blood to ice, my limbs to stone.

And yet my heart, my heart would not stop beating,
Though broken into pieces by your flight.
And so I lived, although the earth seemed spinning
In some dark fearsome void of endless night.

But , as Time ticked and ticked away the minutes ,
Bearing me along within its arms,
So earth brought her delights to lift my senses,
And sought to soothe me with her magic balms.

And thus, what once seemed shattered past all mending
Has somehow come together, and is whole,
And all I ever meant to you, and all you are to me
Are held within the fabric of my soul.

V

More General and Narrative Poems

The Bag Lady

Where has she come from?
Shuffling so slow,
Clutching her rag bags?
Where will she go?
She seems not to know
Or even to care
That people avoid her
And grimace, and stare.
Aged yet ageless
Unburdened by time,
Her powder and paint
Dust, grit and grime.
Her music
Discordant motorway din,
Her treasures all scavenged
From trash in a bin.

Has she no loved ones,
no one to care?
No one to find her?
Nobody there?

Shoes other feet
Have moulded to shape,
Someone's old hat,
Someone's old cape.
Someone's old sweater,
Trousers that cling,
All tied in the middle
With someone's old string.
Dark is her path
With no light from a friend.
Does she pray, every day
She may reach journey's end?

Box... 'neath an archway,
graffiti defiled.
Angels protect her.
Somebody's child.

Warriors

Another soldier has been slain
Upon the battlefield.
Another telegram is sent.
Another casket sealed.
Dear ones, their hearts all broken
Will try to stem the tide
Of grief, by overlaying it
With patriotic pride.

And we, though distant strangers,
Know each beloved face
Through media despatches from
That far off, war torn place.
We learn the regiment and rank,
We know from whence they came.
One great extended family,
We honour every name.

And I think of all the battles fought
With guns and knives and staves,
And all the unknown soldiers laid
In all the unmarked graves.

If you wish...

A blaze of starry diamonds lit the heavens
Above a gently ebbing midnight sea.
And so was cast a shimmering enchantment,
And caught therein, a small and graceful tree.
Which bowed its head in awe and grateful wonder,
And waved its pine-clad branches in delight
As every tiny needle was enfolded
And silvered by a lustrous moonbeam-light.

The little tree, filled up with razzle-dazzle
And happiness and joyfulness and bliss,
Hoped that, though the magic flee with dawning,
'Twould be again as beautiful as this.

Ah then, an angel leant down low and whispered
That one day, one day very, very soon
Its branches would be decked with golden tinsel
And baubles shining bright as any moon.
Then it would be wrapped in love and laughter,
Eclipsing icy splendour from afar,
And, best of all… a crowning touch of glory
On topmost branch, a blessed Christmas star.

Wrinkles...

I'm learning to live with my wrinkles.
I don't seem to mind them at all.
There's no sense in sighing for blossom
The calendar tells me it's fall!

For spring is the time to awaken,
To grow, and start leaping about.
And summer is packed full of beauty
And strength, and the absence of doubt.
By autumn, the sunlight has mellowed ,
And days are distilled into wine.
The ripe fruits of life have been tasted
...And some of them pickled in brine.
God willing, ahead lies the winter
(With yet still more stress on the skin),
But I'll be content, if each furrow
Is lit by a glow deep within.

A brow that is smooth may be lovely ,
A face free of lines can be fair,
But, friend, do not fret over wrinkles,
For often, 'tis love puts them there.

Written in the stars

I looked to the stars, the faraway stars,
To the planets, the lantern-light moon,
And searched for answers quite unseen
In the daylight dazzle of noon,
Eyes brim full of starshine,
Mind illumined too,
Somehow in that instant there
I absolutely knew
A truth so big and beautiful,
Magnificent and grand.
And yet so very simple
Little creatures understand.
That Love in all its guises,
All the take and all the give,
Is the rainbow coloured reason
For this life we choose to live.

Gift of Love

There is a love that's way beyond the telling
Past the understanding of the brain.
Bringing all the joys that life can offer,
A constant rainbow, shining through the rain

For, when one heart is gifted to another,
Throughout all light and dark, and time and space,
There never can be loss or separation.
Eternity is breached in that embrace.

Pages...

Dawn was laced with silver
And the moon still graced the sky,
As earth lay hushed and waiting
For a waking bird to fly.
Within a heartbeat time had turned
The page of life to show
A pristine sheet, on which to scribe
The day's swift ebb and flow
Of life and death and joy and pain
As light and dark entwine.
And where each soul on earth will write
Their signature with thine.

The Healer

Close-wrapped in night's dark, all-embracing cloak,
Shy Dawn lay unaware, and late a-bed.
And all seemed shrouded veiled, as though bereft.
The heavy morning mist inlaid with lead.

Until one tiny, feathered lion heart,
Calling kin and comrades to the fray
With music sweet enough to pierce the gloom,
Challenged all that dark, and won the day.

Oh, could those notes but echo round the earth,
Their golden tones must render discord dumb
And cleave through hurt and hunger and despair,
And light the darkness and let healing come?

Masque

As dawn's first light peeped over the horizon
There were Angels in the air and on the wing,
And tho' each wore the garb of thrush or blackbird,
I knew 'twas mere disguise... I heard them sing

Black Velvet

When night has slipped her velvet arms about me
And carried me across the bridge of sleep,
To realms where dreams create a moving landscape
And memories may surface from the deep.

'Tis then I meet those dear and best belovéd
No longer seen in daytime's harsher light.
There, doors swing open to a new dimension,
And comfort holds the heart, and grief takes flight.

Understanding

They're talkin' on the telly,
Each time I press the switch,
Of wars and awful conflicts
Around the world, the which
Cause death and devastation
And agony and fear...
Civilians are dying...
But, oh, my dear, my dear...
'Twas ever thus, since man first learned
To think and talk and stand,
And hold a club and then believe
That he could own the land.
From 'Annibal to 'Enery
Crusaders to the Celts,
Marchin' in their uniforms,
Their armour, woad, and pelts ,
Pillaging and raping ,
And putting to the flame,
All for "just and valid cause",
Or in somebody's name.
For war's some 'orrid octopus

A-lurkin' in its lair ,
Reachin' out to crush the life
From all that's good and fair.
Spreadin' evil tentacles
O'er earth and sea and sky,
Deaf to pleas for mercy or
To babe or mother's cry.
You'd think we'd understand by now
It aint a bit o' good
To rain destruction on the earth
It simply turns to mud,
Which mires heart and mind and soul
In grief and pain and... well...
I aint no theologian but
To me it looks like Hell!
We've simply got to cotton-on,
That like, or like it not,
This blesséd little planet is
The only one we've got.

Tomorrow

For love like ours would monarchs pay
And peasants toil and angels pray.
Two hearts as one, soulmate and lover,
Each incomplete without the other
As night deprived of day.

Alone am I now, and bereft,
And only yesterday is left.
Dear memories, a tapestry
Woven close, by you, for me,
With love and pain the warp and weft.

But this my comfort, this I know,
For Time decrees it must be so...
One day, my spirit, ageless, free,
Will be... wherever yours may be
And all tomorrows grow.

Togetherness

We whisper soft "I love you"
To those dear ones gone before,
And picture them with arms flung wide
Upon some distant shore.
Held within a loving light
On misted golden sands,
And yearn to reach across the void
To clasp those outstretched hands.

And though, with heavy heart, we see
Them set apart, too far,
Beyond all time and space and past
The highest, brightest star,
It is not so, for if we look
With wise eternal eyes,
We know such segregations are
Illusions, cosmic lies.

For all that is, and all that was
And all that may well be,
Combine within the here and now

To set the spirit free.
So loving hearts may ever meet,
And loving thoughts entwine.
There is no separation...
As the water turns to wine.

True Love

A lover may leave you drowning in tears,
Lost and adrift and a prey to your fears.
Used, abused and thrown away,
Fearing the night and hating the day.

Friends and colleagues who smile to your face,
May trample you down, in the upward race.
Then plunge a knife right into your back.
...The boss might simply give you the sack!

And children can cease to be ever a joy
If, using a clever and devious ploy,
They squander the little you've salted away,
Then turn their backs when you're old and grey.

But a four-footed friend, all covered in fur,
With a wonderful woof or a magical purr,
Just comes with love of the purest kind.
Their only betrayal... to leave you behind.

When time decrees they must sicken and die,
And all that is left is to say goodbye ,
When the breath is stopped, and you're torn apart
'Tis then, ah then, that they break your heart.

Thinking of you...

It isn't your birthday or Christmas.
Nothing exciting like that.
No reason to lay the red carpet,
Nor even shake out a pink mat!
Just a collection of hours
Comprising an average day,
And that's why it's perfect for sending
This card and this verse, just to say
That noontime or morning or evening,
Should you feel a tweak or a tug,
That's simply my thoughts wrapping round you
To give you a bit of a hug.
For, though miles apart, we are bonded
With friendship's invisible glue
So when correspondence is tardy,
Remember I love you, I do.
You're always right there in my thinking,
Part of my heart and my mind.
Tho' time may be reckless and heedless,
Blessings and memories bind.
So I'm praying you're healthy and happy.
I'm hoping your day is well starred,
And I'm sending it off, sealed up with an X,
This all-the-time, every-day card.

The Thief

I'm a robber, a thief, a purloiner.
There now, I've said it, it's true.
In fact, I'm a serial offender,
It's "me", it's something I do.

I take every chance that I'm offered,
Any time, any place, any date.
I'm honing my skills by the minute,
Though I say it myself... I am great.

Well it's there, don't you see, it's on offer,
Whilst the world dashes by, in great haste.
So really, I'm doing a service,
Preventing such profligate waste.

But I fancy you will not condemn me
When you know what it is that I steal,
So gather around... come in a bit closer
My trophies I'll gladly reveal.

Alas, there's no cache I've been hiding,
No tangible objects to find,
But, oh, there's abundance of treasures
Locked up in the vaults of my mind.

A riot of rambling roses
Scenting the air with their smile,
A cobweb encrusted with dewdrops
Festooning a fence for a while.

White surf breaking high over granite,
Poppies, like jewels, in corn ,
A daisy just being a daisy,
Sweet birdsong beguiling the dawn.

A vast panoply of sensations
I've taken and stored them away,
Lest all be unnoticed, unheeded and lost,
And the world become silent and grey.

Tessie

...a love song...

You walked beside me and you lit my way.
With your bright presence, what more can I say?
For how can I describe that loving bond
Which bound us heart to heart, and then beyond
To realms none but the blest can comprehend,
Dear best-belovéd, true and faithful friend.
No need for words, devotion in your eyes,
In proffered paw, in small contented sighs.
So, hour by hour, and year on year, it grew
That treasure trove of love 'twixt me and you.

But now the scales are tipped, with dues to pay.
No more our good companionship each day,
For you lie sleeping, 'neath the grassy mound
Just by the gate, and well within the sound
Of breakers washing o'er the sandy beach,
Where wildly scented roses bend and reach
Around, to shield you from the wind and rain and snow.
And deep within my broken heart, I know

That somehow, through dark mists of grief and pain,
Love must survive and find its own again.

'Tis said that when we speak, the spirit hears,
So I'll not spoil your rest with bitter tears.
Instead, until swift time brings kind redress,
May gentle angels hold you close...
"Goodnight... Sweet dreams... God bless".

Tears...

These are not the bitter tears of pain
Which salt the earth, where you lie wrapped in sleep.
But rather, drops of gratitude and joy
That, out of earth and sky and deepest deep
Our stars should meet, and kindle there a flame
To light the heavens past the bounds of time.
And show that life and death and all therein
Are merely coloured trappings of make-believe and mime.
And as I weep, I feel you drawing near
To hold my heart until our souls rejoin.
For joy and pain, perchance, must ever be
The mirrored sides of each new-minted coin.

Time and Tide

Our life's but a wave
Which greets the shore
In fleeting embrace,
Then ebbing becomes
The ocean once more.

Symbiosis

Dearest, I am standing close beside you,
Near as earthly darkness will allow,
Trying so to light your inner being
And bring to you the understanding how
To loose the chains which bind us close in shadows
Deep inside the cavern of despair.
For, tho' you feel bereft and solitary
Be assured, sweetheart, that I am there.
For love will seek its own across the ether,
Striving hard to comfort and uplift.
Saddened then to find that the beloved
Can't comprehend, nor yet accept the gift.

So come, dear heart, look out beyond this prison
And glimpse the rainbow shining up above,
Then, taking all your strength and all your courage
Let me go and bless me with your love.
Thus I will be one with all creation,
Part of every day and every night.
Threaded through the tissue of existence,
Tho' to mortal senses, out of sight.

Yet you will know that this is just illusion
For, in the letting go, you'll surely find
That there is no such thing as separation,
As I live in your heart and soul and mind.

The Home Straight

The days are getting shorter now,
The sun is not so high.
The grass which grows across the fence
Is yellowed, and quite dry.
Sweet Youth looks very young indeed,
Yet also rather wise.
And Eternity seems nearer than
The wide and empty skies.

The images are not so sharp,
All sounds are turned down low.
Yet colours hold a vibrancy,
A deep and inner glow.
The heart of Life beats slowly, like
A velvet-muffled drum,
And years a-waiting in the wings
May simply never come.

Yet everything has settled down
Into its rightful place
Within the Universal Arms.
And I am touched by Grace.

When you wish...

Night was wrapped within her velvet mantle.
All was still, the air as sweet as balm.
No creature footfall broke the silken silence,
No breath of breeze disturbed the sacred calm.
So there I stood, beneath that blaze of glory,
And looked from north to south, from east to west,
And wished on every star within the heavens
That you be healed and whole, dear heart, and blest.

The Lesser Spotted Soul

I've no idea of the shape of my soul.
Does it have any structure at all?
Is it as wide as I am wide
And tall as I am tall?
Does it mirror my bodily outline,
Or is it a wisp, without form?
Is it buffetted by my emotions,
Or calm as the eye of the storm?
Is it hard, is it soft, is it spongy?
Does it think, does it move, does it feel?
Does it sometimes take a vacation,
And hey, come to that, is it real ?

'Tis only at its departing
The soul may be spotted, and then
Revealed as a heavenly body
And therefore... beyond mortal ken.

All the Time in the World

All of the strands of creation are spun
Into infinite spirals of time,
Rotating around in the universe
Heedless of tick or of chime.
Catching each tiny vibration
Sounded by planets and stars,
Hearing humanity's heartbeat ,
Smoothing the deepest of scars.
Endlessly moving, untrammelled
By transient joys or alarms.
While the hopes and the fears of tomorrow
Soon whirl within yesterday's arms.

Special

Everyone is somebody to someone,
Really there's no arguing with that.
Maybe it's your dog who thinks you're gorgeous,
Or failing that, the goldfish or the cat.
Perhaps it is the lady on the checkout,
The one you complimented on her smile,
Or else the person feeling rather lonesome
With whom you stopped and chatted for a while.
Maybe there are folk who've never met you
Grateful that you cared enough to give,
And don't forget the snail plucked from the pathway
And set upon the grass that it might live.
Everyone is special, that's the message,
That is all I really want to say.
Never doubt your power or your glory,
Somehow you are making someone's day.

Rainy Days

The rain it rained, then rained again, and then it rained some more.
It quite outstayed its welcome, in fact, became a bore.
A week ago, the cheery sun looked set to stay a while,
But then it met an isobar, and turned and ran a mile.
'Fraid of being all washed out, diluted, even drowned,
It may not show its face again till autumn comes around.
I'm telling you, I'd had enough. My teeth began to grind
Until I saw a little scene which quite restored my mind.
For there he stood, a sparrow, all set to chirp and sing,
Knee-deep in a puddle and as happy as a king.

Snowdrop

Beneath the tangled branches
Of a lonely, leafless shrub
Held fast within the icy grip of earth,
A tiny little shoot has braved
The dark, and made a stand
For hope and joy and beauty and rebirth.

Sky-Borne

Today the morning sky was thronged with angels,
Their wings spread wide and white against the blue,
And tinted here and there with gleams of glory
Where early-rising sunbeams filtered through.

I knew that they were there to guard and guide me,
No matter what the tenor of the day.
Close to me in happiness and laughter,
Closer still when edges start to fray.

There's times when I may find a pure white feather,
Or sense their nearness in a whispered sigh,
Or simply feel my spirits gently lifted.
But oh today… today, they filled the sky .

Sketches

"Live life at speed."
That was my creed.
I burned the gas
To swerve and pass.
I felt the power,
Lived for the hour.
My field of play
The motorway.
I didn't know
The tyre would blow
I didn't know...

I joined the group,
Jumped through each hoop,
Was swept along
By fervour's song.
Forgot to think,
Became a link.
No give and take,
Just make or break.
I didn't know

How hate could grow,
…I didn't know…

We fell in love,
Fit like a glove.
I thought you mine
For all of time.
Then cracks appeared.
We snarled and sneered.
As rifts grew wide
I hugged my pride.
I didn't know
I'd miss you so
…I didn't know…

Sights Unseen

Oh mother can you see them,
The tiny elfin folk?
Dancing round a fairy fire
With rainbow-coloured smoke.
See their queen, in dewdrop crown
And pansy petal cloak
Wave her wand and cast a spell
In one star-spangled stroke.

No child, my eyes are blinkered
For I wear an adult's yoke.

Oh mother, see the children
Who come to play with me.
Some of them have lived before,
And some are yet to be.
And in our land of make-believe
We sail an endless sea
Always making sure we're home
Again in time for tea.

Alas that childhood door is locked
And I have lost the key.

Oh mother, see the angels
Spread wings across the skies,
Beautiful and loving
And wonderful and wise.
Linked to everyone on earth
By shiny golden ties,
Cradling our hopes and dreams,
Our laughter and our sighs.

Oh yes, my child, I see them all...
I see them in your eyes.

Seagulls

Gulls wildy wheeling and calling,
Riding rough waves and skimming the sea,
Catching the wind and soaring... soaring
Nearer to heaven than I'll ever be.

Seasons

There was a time when
You were all my life
My waking thought, my daily bread,
Possessing heart and soul and head.
My hope, my fear. My deity.
My now and my eternity.
Spring fever running rife.

A time when
Love could do no wrong.
For sweet, swift hours were dream imbued,
And all the world was rainbow hued.
Stars shed luminescent lights
O'er wild, impassioned, scented nights.
While earth sang summer's song.

A time when
The carousel stood still.
And only silent music played.
Indifference crept in... and stayed.
Loves chains gave way to rusty key,

The coloured leaves fell off the tree,
And autumn's winds blew chill.

Now comes a time when
Blood runs cold and thin.
And solitary steps admit
Twilight hours are lonely lit.
Harsh Time cleaves furrows on the brow.
I would not have you see me now,
As winter closes in.

Saints Alive

I wonder, can you help me please?
I'm looking for a saint.
Someone who has virtues which
Most other people aint.
Filled top to toe with goodness,
Doing everything they ought,
Who never speaks an unkind word
Or thinks a naughty thought.
Always kind and patient,
Never tired or cross,
Or grumpily exclaiming that
They couldn't give a toss!

Alas! My search is fruitless
No matter how I try…
It seems the purely pristine
Are in very short supply.
And, should you think you've met one
Walking on their saintly way,
Please look closely at their feet…

You may see bits of clay.
For now, in truth, I'm thinking that
There must be saints galore,
Living here amongst us and
Like as not, next door.

Offering a helping hand
And kindly listening ear,
And smiles to light a gloomy day,
And little gifts to cheer.
They rise above the daily round
Of toil and fear and woe.
(But never flash a halo
So that you'd never know)
Living life as best they can,
Feet firmly on the ground.
...All too human part-time saints...
They're everywhere around.

Welcome Home

May this be a happy home,
Filled with love and light,
With walls so strong and roof so sound
It holds you snug and tight.

May doors and windows open wide
To friends and kith and kin,
With promise of a warm embrace
For all who enter in.

And may its energies inspire,
Its aura bring sweet rest.
And may it be a haven
For your heart. And angel blest.

Rushing along...

There are so many folks on the pavement,
All dashing here, going there.
Some looking happy and eager,
Others quite burdened with care.
Each one absorbed in emotions
Swirling in head and in heart,
Part of a crowd and yet seeming
Lost, in a world set apart.
Thinking up schemes for a million,
Dreaming of making ends meet,
All rushing off to that "somewhere",
Just past the end of the street.
Do any among them, I wonder,
In all of this hurrying throng,
Hear the high notes of a blackbird
Blessing the day with a song?

Rescue

A time there was when dread and fear possessed me,
Their icy fingers clasped around my heart,
As I was cast adrift into the darkness,
Lacking compass, guiding star or chart.
And there, and in that state, I might have perished,
Having no resources of my own,
Carried by relentless tidal currents
To sink, with scarce a ripple, like a stone.
But hands reached out, and arms clasped round about me,
And hearts embraced and heads were bowed to pray,
As countless little acts of love and kindness
Warmed the world and gently lit my way.

Rainbow

We cannot know, my love, I fear
What lies ahead... a smile... a tear,
Despair or hope or joy or woe
Or life or death. We cannot know
How straight the path we'll tread together
This year, next year, sometime, never.

So let us pause. Come, take my hand,
For I must make you understand
How very dear you are to me.
You woke my mind and set it free.
You held my heart, a stone cold thing,
And gave it warmth and made it sing.

You coaxed the sunbeams out to play
And chased my shadows clean away.
You turned my darkness into light
And lit the moon and stars at night.
You took the pieces... made a whole
And put a rainbow in my soul.

Quiet Time

I rose very early one morning ,
Whilst everyone slumbered and dozed .
And even the daisies lay fast asleep,
Their pinkly-fringed eyelashes closed.
And I walked for a while on the clifftops
Which border the sand and the sea,
Lost in a peace which enfolded
A wildness of rabbits and me.

Present Company

I do not walk alone
For I am thronged about
With memories, and know
That those who shared awhile
My lifetime's path
Are very near. They flow
Like dappled sunlight
On a constant stream
Throughout my heart and mind.
They soothe my soul.
And so, with passing years
I am resigned
To shadows... echoes...
And to music played
In soft, nostalgic tone.
And tho' I may well seem
In solitary state, appearances deceive.
I do not walk alone.

Had I the power...

Had I the power, I'd take your pain
And soak it in soft summer rain,
To rinse away that bitter taste
Which lays each new day's hope to waste.

Had I the power, I'd free your mind
From lonely darkness, so you'd find
That all around, within your grasp
Are strong, uplifting hands to clasp.

Had I the power, I'd hold your heart,
And, with a master healer's art
Mend all the wounds and hurts, and then
Light it up with love again.

Had I the power, I'd make you whole
In body, mind and heart and soul.
Had I the power, the power divine
To gift a life... I'd give you mine.

Playmates

Once upon a time ago,
Or so I have heard tell,
A band of fairies fluttered forth
From their enchanted dell.
They flew o'er hills and dales and woods
Through meadows and by streams,
And gathered in some moonbeams,
And spun some happy dreams.
They looked and looked about them
Hoping they would find
Animals and children
Or other giant kind.
And when, at last, they chanced to meet
They had such happy fun
Dancing round the dewdrops
Or snoozing in the sun.
And all the fairies promised
They would come again quite soon.
Then, mixing spells together
With a daisy-petal spoon,
They scattered drops of magic

Round and round about
So animals and children
Need never have a doubt
That whether it is raining
Or whether it is fine
Those who seek for sprites and such
Are sure to see a sign.
There may not be a rustling
Or e'en a tinkly sound,
But where there is a fairy ring
Those wee folk are around.

Adornment

At close of day, I pulled the heavy curtains,
And trod, with weary feet, upon each stair.
Whilst winter's moonlight silvered starry heavens
Illuminating landscapes stark and bare.

When morning came, I drew apart the drapings
To find enchantment dancing in the air.
For gentle night had clothed the earth in diamonds
And dawn had tied pink ribbons in her hair.

Patterns

We are individual patterns, worked
With different coloured threads.
And myriads of thoughts abound
In multitudes of heads.
Each one of us is special,
With no two quite the same,
Tho' all are equal players in
Life's wondrous, cosmic game.
Swept along by passions
Of love and hate and wrath,
Forgetting we are cut and sewn
From universal cloth.

For everything that lives and breathes,
That flies or swims or stands,
Is made of fibres crafted by
The Master Weaver's hands.
And being thus encompassed,
With nothing set apart,
A butterfly may rock the earth
As mankind breaks her heart.

Oh God...!

I do not understand a god
Whose fixed and iron will
Decrees that faithful followers
Must hurt and maim and kill.
I do not understand a god
Who twists the heart and mind,
Demanding slavish duties from
The blind, led by the blind.
A god who's quick to take offence,
To blame, to hold a grudge.
Bereft of all compassion
And a swift and cruel judge.

A god like that could only spring
From man's poor little brain,
Obsessed with power and progress,
And all things trite and vain.
Ignoring simple truths which all
The sacred writings hold,
That love alone unlocks the code,
Which turns the base to gold.

So Man must make his destiny,
Be that for good or ill,
For he accepted long ago
A precious gift... free will...

To walk the path of vengeance
And bigotry and blood
And hell-fire and damnation,
Famine, fire and flood.
Or else to take the upward road,
Which sets the self apart
And leads, through understanding
To love's creative heart.
If we could just aspire to be
As god-like as we can,
Instead of making the divine
Resemble paltry man...

Then, perhaps, and only then
Would wars and conflicts cease,
And earth draw breath, and sing at last
Of universal peace.

One o'clock, two o'clock...

He stood tall and straight in the grass,
Head held erect and so proud.
A somewhat antique dandelion
With hair like an aureole cloud.
When the hand of fate fell upon him
(Wrapped up in a three-year-old fist)
Plucking him up and holding him high,
He welcomed his ultimate tryst.
As, helped by a huffing and puffing
Seeds lifted up and away,
Scattering promised renewal of life,
To the chant of the time of the day.

No Man's Land

I sit alone
On barren rock
In no man's land ,
And watch
Life's blossoms wither
In the arid sand.

Kind hands reach out
But all in vain.
They beat the air.
And Hope stands by
To leap across,
But does not dare.

No sight, no scent,
No touch, no sound
Can reach me here,
For I am bound.
In thrall to black
Constricting fear.

And yet I must
Find courage now
To stir and stand,
Lest your brave heart
Should join with mine
In no man's land.

Night Terrors

There are screeches, there are whistles
There is *bang... bang... bang.*
And it seems as though the universe is cursed.
And I'm looking for a place where I
Can *hide, hide, hide,*
My heart is beating fast enough to burst.
There's flashes and explosions
And there's fire, fire, fire.
Every instinct urges me to flee.
I'm hoping and I'm praying it will
Stop... stop... stop,
Please will someone, somehow, rescue me.
The darkness has been stolen
It is gone, gone, gone,
Replaced by a cacophony of light.
No one seems to hear me, as I
Scream, scream, scream,
Please... let there be an end to Bonfire night .

Treasure Hunt

I've made some resolutions,
And guess that you have too,
Though some will soon be broken
Beyond the aid of glue.
But here I've one that's special
Freshly made today,
And filled so full of joy, I'd like
To share it, if I may.

OK then, are you ready?
It's a simple little thing…
Just that we must be alert
To catch a glimpse of wing,
The twinkle of a wand, or e'en
A tiny tinkly sound,
For these are signs to tell us
That the fairies are around.

No matter what the weather,
Throughout the days and nights,
Fairies clad in gossamer

And elves in grass green tights,
Gnomes all wearing gum-boots
And pixies in their hats
Are dashing, hither-thither ,
Or sitting down for chats.

Scattering enchantment
And magic everywhere,
Weaving rainbow ribbons
Through Mother Nature's hair.
Spinning cheery chuckles
Putting gloom to flight,
Polishing the glo-worms
To liven up the night.

I'm quite resolved to see them
Somehow, sometime, somewhere,
And step right into fairyland
And all the wonders there.
I'm sure I'll get my heart's desire,
My dreams will all come true.
And, oh my friends, this bright new year,
I wish the same for you.

By any other name...

It grew midst the grass, by the roadside,
And could have been flower or weed.
Did it start life planted and tended?
Or spring from a wind-carried seed?

The petals were lilac and purple,
The leaves quite the mossiest green,
And it stood there surrounded by daisies
All dusted with dew-misty sheen.

A weed or a flower? What matter?
For all interact, play a part,
And names lead to classifications
Whilst beauty speaks straight to the heart.

Morning Glory

I walked within a world of wondrous colours,
Of errant rainbows turning heaven's key,
As softest saffron swept the far horizon
And rosy seagulls roamed a sapphire sea.
The sands were paved with gold and lit with diamonds,
The air was chilled champagne... and all for me.
And all for all abroad this glory morning,
A winter's gift to set the spirit free.

Mother of Pearl

You'll know what I mean when I say there are folk
We meet on our journey through life,
Who seem to be there with the purpose and aim
Of causing us trouble and strife.
No matter how hard we try to stay calm,
They wriggle right under the skin,
And "rising above it" has not got a chance
'Cos brother, you aint gonna win!
They'll argue until the cows come home
That black is undoubtedly white ,
And they won't take a journey to Timbuktu…
Though you'd gladly stump up for the flight.
They proffer their cast-iron views on things
From the price of fish to taxation,
And, putting it bluntly, they're simply a pain
In the neck… or some other location!
They always cause your hackles to rise
By rubbing your fur the wrong way,
Then tread on your corns and heedlessly make
Each nerve-end unravel and fray.
But… life has a habit of working things out,

And we see, as the years unfurl,
That, but for those "irritants" doing their job,
We'd never turn into a pearl.

Mirror Image

I've no idea who she can be
Nope… no idea at all.
That ancient, stooped and withered crone
Who just walked down the hall.

She must have come in by mistake.
I'd best ask for her name.
I glimpsed her in the mirror and
…We're both dressed just the same!

It's such a shame she's old and bent,
But still, I fail to see
What business she has here, because
She's naught to do with me.

For age has left me quite unscathed,
E'en though the years have fled.
I'm still the girl I always was
…At least… inside my head.

Millie's Gift

There is a love that's way beyond the telling.
Past the understanding of the brain.
Bringing all the joys that life can offer,
A constant rainbow, shining through the rain.

For, when one heart is gifted to another ,
Throughout all light and dark, and time and space,
There never can be loss or separation.
Eternity is breached in that embrace.

Me?

It really comes as quite a shock
And dims my rosy glow,
Whene'er I write my date of birth
...It seems so long ago!

It can't be right. It isn't me.
There's something badly wrong.
The years are simply whizzing by
Where once they lingered long.

I exercise and moisturise
To keep things taut and tight,
But gravity is pulling hard
And may well win the fight!

And yes, I creak and groan a bit
When trying to uncoil,
But all machinery, betimes
Can use a drop of oil.

So I'll not go for Botox jabs,
Or toil in high-tech gym,
Nor liposuck my fat away
To make me slinky slim.

A wrinkle here, a furrow there
Are no real cause for strife,
For they are simply records
Of the many gifts of life.

And deep inside my head and heart
Where no one else can see,
Appearances don't matter much,
For there, I'm simply me.

And if that "me" has used the years
To love and give and grow,
Then I'll not fuss, for in the end
That's all that counts, you know.

Magic

If I could find a magic wand
I'd wave it in the air,
And cast a spell to take away
All fear and pain and care.
I'd clear the dark and stormy clouds,
Revealing skies of blue,
And smooth the rocks which mar the path
For you and you and you.
I'd feed the starving, heal the sick
And bid all conflicts cease,
So every heart could feel awhile
The blessed balm of peace.

But wands, alas, are hard to find.
I don't have one to hand,
And dreams of solving worldly ills
Are spun of shifting sand.
So each must use the stuff of life,
The losses and the gains,
To weave a rainbow-coloured robe,
Or heavy leaden chains.

And, toiling thus, from day to day,
Assuredly we'll find
The magic's in the mixing
Of the heart and soul and mind.

Love is...

Love is...
A brown egg, boiled soft. Toast soldiers, cut thin
Ready and waiting, with spoon, to dip in.
A "Yes" or a "No". A "Maybe... we'll see."
A line full of washing. Trifle for tea.
A wild waggy tail. A nudging wet nose.
Laughter and weeping. A single red rose.
Train sets and teddies. Fluorescent socks,
A lifetime of memories stored in a box.
Half - licked ice lolly, dipped in the sand
Joyously proffered by hot sticky hand.
Scrimping and saving. Ends made to meet.
A new pair of shoes, for a new pair of feet.
A heart near to breaking. Hope soaring high.
Knee kissed all better. Hot apple pie.
Marks on the wall to see how they grow,
Living and learning. Letting them go.
Passionate kisses, a tender caress.
A hot water bottle.
Goodnight and God bless.

Love...

Love is...
Fragile as cobwebs,
Tempered as steel.
Fabric of dreamtime,
All that is real.
Desired beyond diamonds
Yet freely bestowed,
Light to illumine
Life's perilous road.
Small glow of comfort,
Beacon of hope,
Reason for tying
A knot in the rope.
Giving, forgiving
Whatever the cost,
A haven awaiting
The lonely and lost.
Raising the heart
With magical leaven.
Song of the earth,
Echo of heaven.

Light Fantastic

Walking on a sunlit-morning beach
All wave imprinted by the ebbing tide,
With here and there a small and rocky pool
Where tiny creatures still could swim and hide.
I saw, some way ahead, a disc of gold,
Seemingly just waiting there for me.
I hurried forward, eager to discern
What this treasure trove could really be.
Then I saw it was, in truth, a stone,
Round and unremarkable and grey,
And yet transformed, transmuted by the touch
Of early-rising sunbeams here today.

And musing then upon the alchemy
Which I had surely witnessed taking place,
I hoped that I too might reflect the light
And so be beautiful, and touched by grace.

Left Behind...

Why did you go without me?
How could you leave me so?
In a world without substance or meaning,
Where time has forgotten to flow.

Left me to waste and to wither,
Adrift in this arid domain,
Where the signposts spell out "Desolation",
"Despair", and "Intractable Pain".

With no hope of rescue or comfort,
No prospect of joy or of cheer.
For these were all bound in your being,
And you... are not here... are not here...

I've searched for you, waking and sleeping,
Silent, and calling your name,
Until every star in the heavens
Reflects back and echoes my pain.

So all that is left, is to linger,
And act out the rest of the play,
Creeping towards the finale
Day... after day... after day...

I did not know...

I did not know that I was just existing
Throughout the days and years that make up time.
Tho' I had trekked for miles o'er barren landscapes,
Playing out a harsh charade, a mime

I did not know, as I walked in the shadows
That, far beyond the clouds, lay sunlit air.
I did not know that paradise existed,
Nor ever dreamed that I might sojourn there.

I did not know my life was bleak and bankrupt.
I'd given all and heeded not the cost.
And, dearest heart, until you came and found me,
I did not even know that I was lost.

Jim

One man and his dog.

I'd like for you to meet my mate
Goes by the name of Jim.
I got him from a sanctuary
As kindly took him in.
They rescued him from off the streets
Where he was sleepin' rough,
But nobody adopted him
For he was not "enough".
Not tall enough or short enough,
Not 'andsome, awful thin,
And parts of him was pitiful
With sores and broken skin.
But soon as I clapped eyes on him
I somehow knew that he
Would be my good companion.
Yes… He would do for me.
And by my side he's been since then,
Stuck fast as superglue.
I've never known a love so strong

Nor heart so brave and true.
'Course, there are times we disagree,
Like when I'm in a rush
And he decides to stop and sniff
At every bloomin' bush.
And sometimes when I settle down
And try to watch the match,
He'll see that ruddy football and
Decide it's time to "Catch!"
But when we beg to differ,
Instead of getting tense
We use a bit o' give and take...
It's only commonsense!
We're goin' for a walk now,
Before we have our tea.
I've got a bit of stewing steak
To share 'twixt 'im and me.
And as we make our promenade
To keep us fit and trim,
I wish the whole wide world could be
Best pals... like me... an' Jim.

I wish for you...

A palette of pinks
In a morning sky,
The sound of the sea
On the shore.
Sweet weaving of dreams
As the years go by.
Peace in the midst of war.
Perennial hope
As the seasons change,
Joy in your heart, and to spare.
A warming glow
Through an open door.
A breeze and a course set fair.
Your very own star
To lighten your way,
Friendship wherever you roam.
Renewal of strength
With the dawn of each day,
And angels to welcome you home.

Incarnation

If I had never walked upon this planet
And breathed its air and listened to its song.
If I had never marvelled at a snowflake
Or watched a stream meandering along.
If I had never come to love its creatures
And learned of life and death and of rebirth,
Then would my soul be smaller, weaker, poorer,
If I had never walked upon the earth.

If I had never walked with those who hurt me,
Faced cruelty and ignorance and fears,
However could I comprehend forgiveness,
Or learn to hope and smile, in spite of tears?
Through injury came comfort, peace and healing,
So dark the path, I learned to look, and see.
Though wounds have healed, the scars remain, and truly
Dear enemy I'm glad you walked with me.

If I had never walked with you, belovéd
What could I know of love's transforming power?
Or imagine how your touch, your smile, your presence

Would gild each magic moment of each translucent hour?
If I'd never heard your heart speak soft to my heart,
Soul talk to soul, the way the angels do…
I would never know that life's much more than living
Belovéd if I had not walked with you.

And so we walk, walk on, one with the other
Through race and creed and dark and light and space
To ride the whirligig of all creation
Until, once more, we find a resting place.
There to tread and turn the wheel together,
Just as we have done since time began,
And strive to grow in grace and understanding,
And one day know the meaning of the plan.

Hope

Bleak winter held me fast within its grasp,
Ice-locked into an unremitting chill.
Harsh, hoary arms crushed out each laboured breath,
Paralysing hope and thought and will.

It seemed that ne'er again would gilded light
Break through that sombre, steely stranglehold,
Nor kindly warmth embrace my glacial heart
To thaw the cold… The raw and bitter cold.

And yet, one day, these dull lack-lustre eyes
Beheld a minor miracle, no less,
With power to break that all-pervading ice
Whilst reaching out, to comfort, cheer and bless.

Assuring me that e'en the bleakest grey
Must cede, in time, to green and gold and blue.
This grace was gifted from the sleeping grass
Where snowdrops grew.

High and Mighty

Did I tell you I've friends in high places?
Oh yes, I assure you, 'tis so.
And though they don't boast of their titles
Or put their credentials on show,
I know, without doubt, they are waiting
To fly to my side when I call,
Bringing a light to the darkness
Raising me up when I fall.
I'm certain and sure they are present.
Steadfast, refusing to budge,
For now and again they leave me a clue
And give me a bit of a nudge.
I may find a fluffy white feather.
(And where there are feathers, there's wings)
Or perhaps get a letter from loved ones
With all of the joy that it brings.
The answer, right there to a problem ,
That feeling I'm never alone,
Finding an object long-ago-lost,
A friend on the end of the phone.
The strength to cope and the lift of hope,
The courage to face any fear
All gifts I bet, so I'll never forget
My highly-placed angels are near.

Guardian

Closer than a heartbeat,
Strong as tempered steel.
Warm as summer sunshine,
Hush, be still, and feel.
Soft, as soft as swansdown,
Gentle as a kiss,
Angel arms enfolding,
Healing light and bliss.

Growing Pains

Were I, perchance, an angel
With a bit of time to spare,
Released from high celestial chores
And giving tender care,
I think that I would settle down
Upon a comfy cloud,
With chocolate and popcorn
(If such treats were allowed.)
And there, upon a giant screen
Of wondrous depth and span
I'd watch, and try to understand
"The Chronicles of Man".
I'd see his struggle to survive
When life was harsh and fraught,
And he must hunt and catch his food
(Before those things were bought.)
I'd see him grow from simple soul
To one equipped to think,
Inventor and philosopher
And scribe with pen and ink.
And then, at last, he'd struggle free
From insular cocoon
Spread out bright wings and soar aloft

To walk upon the moon.
And all of this, it must be said,
Would raise a cosmic cheer.
Not so, alas, the darker scenes
Of misery and fear.
Of slings and clubs and catapults,
And axes made of flint.
Of crossbows and of muskets
And steel with deadly glint.
Of instruments of torture
And poison from the skies.
Of powerful corruption
And greed and lust and lies.
And here's the pity of it all,
(Seen easily from here)
The race 'twixt light and darkness
Is neck and neck, I fear.
And if I were an angel
Well, at that point, I know
I'd leave the soft and fluffy cloud
And quit the picture show.
For, not even an angel
I think it's fair to say
Could bear to watch the ending of
This modern passion play.

Will mankind walk into the light
So that it's soul may thrive?
Or opt instead for darkness, and
Will earth herself survive?

Fugitives

They're ruthlessly rooted from borders,
And never allowed into tubs,
In fact, they're persona-non-grata
In all horticultural clubs .
And so, in a way, they are outlaws,
Unwelcome, unloved and reviled,
Rejected by civilization
They have to survive in the wild.

And yet, these humble outsiders
Have powers both potent and real,
And those who are wise to their secrets
May use them to soothe and to heal.
For now they brighten the byways,
Lighting the earth with their glow.
Where'er a dark corner needs dusting with gold
Be sure dandelions will grow.

But then face to face...

I used to call you enemy
In anger, hate and fear.
And saw, in you, a threat to all
The things which I held dear.
I vowed to fight you to the death
By any means to hand,
To hunt you down and root you out
And tear you from the land.
I held aloft the torch of truth
And marched within its light,
For you were wrong, of course, and I
Was very surely right.

Now standing here together,
On some higher plane, we find
A pattern in the pathways which
The architect designed.
Through deserts, swamps and jungles,
O'er harsh and rough terrain,
Yet leaving gaps to lean across
And reach another's pain.

But pride would not. And only death
Could lift and heal and mend.
And you, whom I called enemy,
I now see true... my friend.

Footsteps...

My footsteps left impressions in the snow
Marking out a chanced, haphazard route.
And I could only hope my feet had not
Crushed some hidden, tender, hopeful shoot.

'Twas then I thought to look back down the years
Filled with joy and sorrow, work and play.
And saw the road as smooth as sea-washed sand,
With only fleeting Time to mark the way.

Remembering my rushing heedless haste,
Head in the clouds, awhirl with plan and scheme,
I think of all the lives my path has crossed...
And pray I did not trample on a dream.

After the Rain

Just after a soft summer shower
I spied him… so still, and so fair,
Midst grasses still sprinkled with raindrops
And magic alive in the air.
Surveying a rainbow-hued puddle,
He sat on a moss-covered log.
A princeling, disguised, masquerading
As a smart little greenly-clad frog.

Friends...

If you should need an angel,
Don't sigh and search the skies.
In truth, they're all about you,
Though often in disguise.

For, knowing that life's burdens
Are sometimes hard to bear,
And seeing too, that we might need
A hand, just here and there

Some providence took pity, and,
As though to make amends,
Scattered Angels on the earth,
And simply called them "friends".

My Friend

You are my friend. I love you.
And I know that you love me.
So close are we I'm certain-sure
Whate'er may come to be,
You will be close beside me,
As you have been from the start,
A star to guide my footsteps
And a haven for my heart.

A love so strong and steadfast,
So pure and high and true
Is only ever found in friends
As wonderful as you.
My anchor and my comfort,
My lantern in the fog,
Though I am only human, you
Are love-on-legs... my dog

.

Discovery

Thick, freezing fog has muffled up the morning,
And stolen all the light from dawn's bright smile.
Yet here, a little diamanté cobweb
Uplifts the day by putting on the style!

Angel Express...

'Twould seem there's a fashion for angels
Of every conceivable sort,
And folk are proclaiming with passion
The blessings these visions have brought.
Some see them as filling the heavens,
Beating the air with their wings.
Whilst others just feel an enfolding,
Holding the heart 'till it sings.

Some swear they're an alien species...
The extra-terrestial kind.
And others declare they are merely
A figment... a trick of the mind.
But , given that Angels are clever ,
And also exceedingly wise,
I think they appear when we need them,
In any and every guise.

And I'm sure that they gather our wishes
The instant we free them to fly,
And whisk them along in the ether,

As swift as the blink of an eye.
So I'll send you a thought every morning,
Courtesy, angel express,
To wrap you around with a Heavenly Hug
And whisper "take care" and "God bless".

New Year's Eve

Whilst church bells chime
Swift sands of time
Build castles, high in the air.
And the heart and the mind
Are briefly inclined
To soar, and inhabit them there.

As memories crowd,
All clamouring loud
Of days which have gone before,
Full of hope and of fear,
It is suddenly clear
We have reached a revolving door.

And, standing again
In that empty frame
To the future, the present, the past,
Illusion's play
Is swept away
Revealing the truth at last.

I am you. You are me
In this great cosmic sea,
In which all creation's afloat
And all pleasures and pains
Are but pearls on the chains
Adorning eternity's throat.

Endurance

My heart rejoiced when first I saw the snowdrops,
Perfect pearls atop a slender stem,
Delicate and beautiful and fragile.
Jewels set in nature's diadem.

Then darkly heavy clouds swept o'er the landscape
And snow fell thickly, blotting out the light,
And cruel winds bowed down each head before them,
Whilst icy hands choked everything in sight.

Yet, when the sun at last reclaimed the power
To melt that blanket down into the earth,
Still the snowdrops stood, their grace and beauty
A testament to hope and to rebirth.

Elixir

Picture a small, stoppered bottle
Brown, the colour of earth,
Filled to the brim with a tincture
Of precious and infinite worth.
The tiniest drop of this liquid
Has powers to make or to break,
To conjure the stars in the heavens,
Or cause sure foundations to shake.
It's touch, anointing a desert
Transforms, bringing beauty to life,
And yet it may twist to a whirlwind
Bearing a heart-rending knife.

What is it, this magical potion?
What alchemy's bottled up there?
The label reads "Purest Essence of Love"
And, "Warning! Please handle with care."

Elemental

Somewhere , within the very deepest deep of me ,
Guarded by the beating of my heart,
There glows a tiny flickering of knowing
That I'm a tiny spark, a living part
Of all this great, pulsating, shining cosmos,
Where energies vibrate and change and grow
In cavalcades of make-believe and magic.
An ever new and never ending show.

A tapestry of light and sound and colour,
Growing and evolving with each strand,
Following a blueprint which could only
Spring from some divine creative hand.
And yet... and here's the marvel, here's the wonder...
In all this vast, amazing panoply,
Each single soul is cherished and beloved
And held in all that is, and is to be.

Point of Departure

It is time... I know, you must leave me,
And the knowing is breaking my heart.
For then I must dwell in a light-less world
Where you have no place and no part.
And where will you go, as I'm holding
That discarded coat which you wore?
Is your light to be snuffed, like a candle?
Or will some spark of you soar
Beyond all the stars in the heavens,
Becoming a part of the whole ?
And will you still know that I love you?
How do I cleave to your soul?

I'd wager my life, just to keep you
Here on the earth by my side,
But death holds the hand with the aces
And cannot be duped or denied.
I know there are angels-in-waiting,
I hear their wings beating the air.
They've opened a portal in heaven
And soon they will carry you there.

Now all that is left is to hold you
Tight-wrapped in a final caress,
Whilst whispering thanks for the life we have shared.
Goodnight, best belovéd, God bless.

Daffodils

I don't know how the earth can turn,
The oceans ebb and flow.
How night can follow on from day
And seasons come and go.
With you not here, a part of them,
Joining in their song,
Filling life with meaning,
Righting every wrong.
You will not greet the summer rose
Or autumn's russet glow,
You will not see the daffodils,
And, oh, you loved them so.

I don't know how my heart can beat,
Poor wounded, broken thing.
I don't know how the sun can shine
Or how the birds can sing.
I don't know how my soul exists
Within this lifeless shell,
Or how much pain it can endure,
These things I cannot tell.

But this I know… 'tis worst of all…
How strange it should be so…
That spring will warm the greening earth,
And daffodils will grow.

Concrete Evidence

Cracked and worn and weathered paving stones,
Their ancient mortar crumbled into dust.
Old broken pots, sweet home to sundry snails,
And long-discarded nails a-rimmed with rust.
A barren place, untended and ignored,
A useless waste of space, as some might say,
And yet 'twas here I met with revelation
And Truth and understanding, yesterday .
For in that poor, benighted, ugly spot
Life had taken root, and held on fast,
Putting forth a shoot, a leaf, a flower,
All unremarked by those who hurried past.
Yet there it grew, a wild and wondrous thing,
Prising heavy concrete slabs apart,
A violet, escaped from copse or wood,
And speaking now directly to my heart.
And so I learned this great and gladsome truth
That even in the harshest, bleak terrain
A seed of hope can lift life's crushing loads
So loveliness may flourish once again.
For only in the darkest times, it seems
Can beauty of outstanding strength and grace
Spring forth from some unknown and hidden deep
To challenge fate and show the world it's face.

Mortal's Combats

I do not wonder that this earth is torn
And sundered limb from limb by grievous strife.
That shadowed streets are schoolrooms, and that minds
Are ruled by drug and drink and gun and knife.
Nor wonder yet that hearts and souls may twist
Within the searing heat of hate and fear,
And families implode , and so destroy
All that once was pure and good and dear.

I know that deep foundations can be rocked.
That heaven's gate may lead instead to hell.
And sores can suppurate and never heal.
I understand... for you have taught me well
And I had rather face dread Hades' hounds
With fangs of fire, to tear a life apart,
Or brave a pit of snakes, or dragon's lair
Than bear these wounds from one who held my heart.

If we, whom love once bound so tight about,
And thought to stay so joined 'till life should cease
Are fractured now, beyond all healing's art...
What hope for all mankind? What hope for peace?

The Burden...

My overcoat has now grown much too heavy,
I find that I can scarce endure the weight.
For what was once a warm and welcome garment
Has turned into a leaden cage of late.

Erstwhile, I strove to keep it in condition
And hoped that it would serve me well and long.
But now I find the cloth too closely woven,
The belt constricting and the seams too strong.

I wish that I could shrug it from my shoulders
And leave it where we walked upon the shore.
For now that you are gone from me, belovéd
I have no wish to wear it any more.

All things bright and...

I have heard it said
By those who believe
They are right in the things which they state,
That an angel stands
At a sentry post
By the heavenly golden gate.

And only for those
With a valid pass
Will he turn the celestial key.
For he has to guard
The elysian fields
From everyday sinners you see.

Of course he will let in
Saints by the score,
And maybe a martyr or two.
While some bright souls
Who are extra good
May earn enough points to get through.

No animals, though,
No birds or fish
May reach this rarefied goal.
These innocent friends
Can't enter because
They are bodies, without any soul.

Well, if that's the case
I'm telling you now
That what I am going to do,
Is step aside
So others may take
My place in that paradise queue.

And having no wish
To lounge around
In vacant and vaulted halls,
I'll pitch my tent
On the open plains
Outside those buttressed walls.

And there with creatures
Great and small
I'll find a sacred space,
For all that lives
And breathes, must hold
A tiny spark of grace.

And by the rules
Of play, laid down
Within this cosmic game,
Each spark will rise
To join at last
The bright eternal flame.

Building Blocks...

Another birthday almost here.
You know, it isn't on
The way the years just roll around
…No sooner here, than gone.

It seems like only yesterday
I rode my bike to school,
And chafed against authority
And every stuffy rule.

How seamlessly the earth revolved,
Revolved, revolved again.
When suddenly, behind my back
Appeared… I know not when,

A wall, built up of decades-worth
Of days and months and years.
Each brick a mix of love and joy,
Of laughter, grief and tears .

This wall is high and wide and long
And, yes, it must be said
That more bricks are accounted for
Than ever lie ahead.

And now, another year has come
To rest the briefest while,
I'll greet it with a cheery wave,
I'll even raise a smile.

And never let the march of time
Be cause for sighs or strife.
Instead, I'll simply carry on
Adventuring through life.

Being...

Wet, shining sands glowed gold
And rippled rose,
Dark, silhouetted seagulls
Clove the air.
Whilst lace-edged wavelets
Wandered round my toes,
And even my dim eyes
Saw heaven there.

Beguiled...

I used to think that I would not grow old,
That time would simply nod, and pass me by.
Mortality and such were not for me,
Though other folk might weaken, ail or die.
The years would never gather up my skin,
Then let it fall, in crêpy pleat or fold,
Nor slowly drain the colour from my hair,
Substituting silver there for gold.

My eyes would never dim, nor hearing fade.
My frame and limbs would aye stand straight and true,
And all those castles floating in the air
Would keep their gilded spires and rainbow hue.

But I was wrong. Sweet youth beguiled my feet
And left me in a paradise for fools.
'Till, treading out the season's changing paths
I learned to play by life's unbending rules.
And now I see the pattern in the weave.
And feel the graining deep within the wood.
For all the while, the wheel of life must turn.
Strong, its pull, and swift and sure and good.

Because...

I have a friend,
Life is never lonesome
Or dark, or cold,
Or lacking laughter's cheer.
For always there's a beam
Of starry light,
By which to chart and steer.
Herein lies wealth,
Though having neither grand estate, nor gold ,
And owing much to thrift,
Make do and mend,
I am content. I have enough.
And more,
I have a friend.

Beauty

I met with mutual friends, the other day,
Who knew us when our days were fresh with dew.
We marvelled at how swift the years had flown,
Taking with them all we meant to do.
They told me that, a month or so ago,
On visiting the city where you dwell,
They'd chanced upon you strolling in a park,
And stopped awhile to chat a little spell.

They said the passing years had used you ill,
Riding roughshod o'er your face and frame,
Taking all and putting nothing back,
Holding all the aces in the game.
Draining smiling colours from your eyes,
Dulling that sharp intellect and wit,
Leaving ashes scattered round your heart
Where once the warmest, brightest flames were lit.

That is what they said. 'Twas their description,
And doubtless they believed they told me true,
But looking deep within the eye of memory

I find you minted fresh and all brand new.
Though winter may cause cracks within the structure,
Make engines slow and systems go awry,
We each have, deep inside, a shining template,
Which earth time cannot touch and passes by.

Autumnal Antics

When we look around about, at hedgerow, shrub and tree,
At all the magic captured there, it's very plain to see
That fairies have been busy… (they're on overtime I guess)
To make sure Mother Nature has a lovely autumn dress.
Rising oh-so-early from a comfy, cozy bed
To paint each single rosehip in the reddest shade of red,
And cuddle up to greengages, apples, pears and plums,
So they will ripen up, becoming food for fairy tums.
They listen to the whisperings of rustly russet leaves
And hang up sparkly cobwebs because they're sure to please,
Then spend a while with baby bats and teach them how to flit,
And scatter gleams of glow around, so all is mellow-lit.

And when their task is over, then the fairies… yes, you've guessed,
Tip-toe off to Dreamland, for a bit of well earned rest.
'Till winter comes, and harshly stamps his foot upon the ground,
Waking them from slumber to hang icicles around.

All Together Now...

Every single second,
Every heartbeat tick of time,
Encapsulates the whole of life
In holographic mime.
Myriad new beginnings
Draw their first expectant breath,
As endings make their exit
In this dance of life and death.

Desert sands. Gentle rain.
Motorway. Country lane.
Crushing loss. Massive gain.
Soaring wings .Rusty chain.

Helping hand. Miser's clutch.
Running wild. Tiny hutch.
Vicious blow. Tender touch.
Mass starvation. Much too much.

Rainbow hopes. Black despair.
Crass neglect. Loving care.
Devastation. All set fair.
Hoard and stockpile. Care and share.

Like the clicking of a shutter,
Or the blinking of an eye,
Each action is recorded ,
Every word and every sigh.
Past the understanding,
Beyond the asking why.
Captured all together
As eternity goes by.

Cast Iron Love

You are woven through the fabric of my being,
Within each heartbeat, and in every breath.
And yet I lack the power to stop you flying
Into the waiting, open arms of death.

I never, ever dreamed I would be standing
Against the onslaught of this anguished fear,
Unable to prevent the devastation
Of all that makes my life worthwhile and dear.

Yet stand I must, and use my fragile courage
To strengthen fledgling wings, before your flight.
And never try to hold you back, with weeping
From soaring out of darkness, into light.

There will be time... an emptiness of longing,
To grieve and keen in mourning's dark refrain.
For now, I'll gird myself in armour plating,
To shield you from the burden of my pain.

Never

Never say you can never forgive
The wounds or the slights or the pains,
For the heart cannot heal
When all it can feel
Is the weight of manacle chains.

Never say you will never move on
From those tortuous crags in your mind,
For the soul cannot breathe
Until it can leave
That desolate landscape behind.

For never and never and never can be
The longest and loneliest time,
And lives laid waste
By a bitter taste
Cannot hear the Angelus chime.

Angels Unaware

Feeling in need of an angel,
I prayed that I might meet a few.
Needn't be Michael or Gabriel…
Your average angel would do.
And then when I peeped through my fingers
Wondering what I might see,
I saw you there standing beside me,
And holding a nice cup of tea.

Just then I was given an inkling
That all may not be as it seems,
For angels are not just in heaven
Or floating around in our dreams.
Instead there are angels-in-secret
Who travel on foot or by car,
Quite unaware of their calling,
They don't even know who they are!

Yet here they are round and about us,
Helping us make do and mend,
Disguised for a time, masquerading

As sweetheart and neighbour and friend.
And some of these everyday angels
May speak in a purr or a woof,
And how did they get their invisible wings?
By loving us, see... that's enough .

Amber's Song

At the end of the day
There is only one thing,
There's only one song
The soul has to sing.
There's only one loss
And there's only one gain,
Only one joy
And only one pain.
There's only one way
To learn how to fly,
One reason for living,
One reason to die.
There's just one compulsion
To kneel and to pray.
It's all about love
At the end of the day.

The Lonely Journey

Each soul must walk alone along life's pathway,
Whilst sojourning upon this spinning sphere,
Tasting bitter dregs and honeyed sweetness,
Feeling joy and hope and pain and fear.
Unaware that this is but an instant
Captured in the swirling mists of time,
So present thoughts may work upon some facet
And cleanse it of accumulated grime.

Though there be other pilgrims on the journey,
Bound into the mind and round the heart
With ties of love, or conflict, or of duty,
The soul must labour onwards quite apart.
Negotiating labyrinthine byways
...With pause to help another, where it can...
Seeking to determine, from the signposts
The destiny of incarnated man.

Learn to see the reaping in the sowing.
The finished house in every hammered nail.
To catch a guiding star and hold its shining,

And know itself the teller and the tale.
Though teachers may impart their wealth of wisdom
And share the wondrous secrets they've been shown,
To reach the peak which leads to understanding
Each soul must climb the mountain on its own.

Angelic Friends

We think of angels soaring high, with wondrous spreading wings,
Wearing golden halos and playing harps and things.
Yet I've been told, yes, gospel truth, been told by those who know,
This ancient view of the angels, must broaden and widen and grow.

For they come in all shapes and all sizes. All textures and colours as well,
As like to be pushing a dust-cart as ringing a heavenly bell.
There are those who declare that to see them, we must train the mind and the heart,
Convinced they are rarefied beings who live in a world quite apart.

And some folk, they see them as aliens, still others as music and light.
But I have a differing viewpoint... and somehow I think that I'm right.
For I look in the eyes of my four-footed friend, and don't have a shred of a doubt,
I feel a Eureka-type moment, and just want to holler and shout.

Some people, both goodly and honest, will "tut", shake their heads and demur,
But I'm telling you, I can see angels... and they're covered in feather and fur.
They're down here and dwelling amongst us, to guide and protect and to love.
(E'en Daniel made friends with a lion, and Noah had faith in a dove!)

They teach us devotion, both tender and true, and demonstrate absolute trust,

And selflessly, gallantly cleave to the side, when everything else turns to dust.
Healing the heart and soothing the soul, with a touch or a look or a song.
Lighting the darkness, smoothing the way and helping the weary along.

A love beyond life
From the purest of hearts,
A welcoming joy, ever new,
Are the gifts which they bring?
So I'm asking you, friend...
That sound like an angel to you?

Advice
for 'Kenzie, Maddie, and Dixie-May

Little girls, draw near awhile
And hear these words I say,
So they may light the way ahead
And shine through every day.
For they are words of wisdom
Which will often spring to mind,
Helping, healing, guiding,
Bringing treasures of a kind.
For each new day's an outline,
Left for you to colour in,
And then to put away and keep.
(It can't go in the bin.)
Nothing there can be erased
So paint with carefulness.
Never put in temper, for
That makes an awful mess.
Add lots of hugs and kisses
To show how much you care,
But fibs are mean and nasty, so
We won't have any there.

Always do the best you can,
Give as well as take.
Find some laughter in each day,
Be kind for goodness sake.
Learn all you can and think and grow,
Be generous and fair.
Look for pathways straight and true
And place your footsteps there.
Cherish Mother Earth and all
Her creatures small and great.
Hold on tight to friendship.
Let go of blame and hate.
Never envy other folk,
Be glad for all you've got.
Remember 'please' and 'thank you'
For they matter such a lot.
Stop and look and listen
There is magic all around.
Try to touch the stars,
But keep your feet upon the ground.
And if ever you are worried
Or scared, or sad or blue,
Just call your guardian angels
And they will help you through.
So, when years roll and take their toll,
As youth ebbs with the tide,
Still… though you're old as Grandmum…
You'll be beautiful, inside.

Photo of a Dear Friend

I saw a photograph of you the other day,
Taken, oh, some many years ago.
You must have been... about sixteen I'd say,
And all alight with youth's intrinsic glow.

Gazing from that sepia-tinted page
You faced the years, advancing one by one,
Not heeding Winter's waiting, grey-meshed cage
Nor worried Spring's bright bloom must soon be gone.

And rightly so. For all that Time could do
To show his footprints marching through the years,
Was mark his presence with a line or two
Recording "Here was laughter", "Here were tears".

That photograph I saw, the other day
Was very lovely but it's day is done.
And I prefer your present countenance,
For all I love in you, is writ thereon.

Feathered Friends

Come, little ones, there's water in the bowl
And here... some crusts of bread, which
I have saved for thee.
Accept these very least of things as thanks
For soaring songs, surrounding
All the earth and me.

Everything Changes

Everything changes,
God made it so.
The hours and the seasons,
The ebb and the flow.
Clouds spill their raindrops,
Earth drinks her fill,
Everything changes,
Nothing is still.

Those we have loved
Who are gone from our sight,
Released from the body,
Transformed into light,
No more may we hold
And caress with our tears,
But love, all enfolding
Illumines the years.

Transcending all time
And all space, and all pain,
Finding the rainbow
Born of the rain.
Starlight to sunrise,
Dewdrops to frost,
Everything changes,
Nothing is lost.

The End